1325 Buddhist Ways
to Be Happy

1325 Buddhist Ways to Be Happy

Barbara Ann Kipfer

Ulysses Press

Published by:
ULYSSES PRESS
P.O. Box 3440
Berkeley, CA 94703
www.ulyssespress.com

ISBN10: 1-56975-587-6
ISBN13: 978-1-56975-587-7
Library of Congress Control Number 2006938933

Printed in Canada by Transcontinental Printing

10 9 8 7 6 5 4 3 2 1

Editor: Mark Woodworth
Cover Design: DiAnna VanEycke
Interior Design: Lourdes Robles

Distributed by Publishers Group West

Table of Contents

INTRODUCTION: BUDDHA'S AND BUDDHIST THOUGHTS ON HAPPINESS

One of the epithets of the Buddha was "The Happy One" (*Sugata* in Pali). You have probably seen many statues and images of the Buddha looking quite calm, but it might be a somewhat unexpected notion that the Buddha was actually a very happy guy. This book gathers the Buddha's thoughts on something we all share—a wish to be happy. Since the Buddha lived almost three thousand years ago, this book also includes passages from those who have studied "The Happy One" as well as from some who have carried on his teachings.

Many spiritual paths focus on attaining happiness through meditation, relaxation, understanding, and awareness. Your spiritual journey begins when you become aware of the suffering that each and every one of us undergoes. This motivates all of us to escape that suffering and find happiness. Achieving freedom from suffering and attaining happiness have always been the ultimate ideal and the working goal of Buddhism and other spiritual philosophies.

The concept of happiness possesses a rich and varied history. Happiness is now an enormously popular topic in books that are offshoots of the branches of philosophy and psychology. Most ancient writings about humans contain in the background a happiness-like concept of well-being and of things working out in a good way. Aristotle's and Plato's treatments of the topic of happiness are much discussed, for example, but far fewer works address the Buddha's teachings and their direct relation to happiness. The Dalai Lama has brought this to our attention with his books. This new book, *1,325 Buddhist Ways to Be Happy,* gathers quotations and passages from the Buddha and his students. Each section incorporates quotes or sayings from Buddhist writings that describe the state of happiness or tell how to obtain it. Taken together, these passages are all about a major theme—happiness—and the guiding words give them even more depth and value.

Tests that involve brain scans reveal that people who meditate and those who are embarked on a spiritual path tend to be happy, calm, and serene people. Using new scanning techniques, neuroscientists have discovered that certain areas of the brain light up constantly in these people, indicating the presence of both positive emotions and a good mood. This happens at times even when they are not meditating or practicing their spirituality. These areas in the left prefrontal lobes are linked to positive emotions, self-control, and temperament.

The Buddha, who was also referred to as "The Happy One," discovered that suffering was not caused by external, traumatic events, but rather by qualities of mind that shape our perceptions and responses to events. Accordingly, the Buddha said that happiness is not to be found in the outer, social world, but in a transformation of mind that generates wisdom, tranquility, and compassion. The more self-centered we become, the less happy we are. Buddhist philosophy focuses on the concepts of "no self" and karma—the discovery that we are not separate from others and that our actions affect everything and everyone. Learning self-forgetfulness is actually the experience of true happiness. The precepts of Buddhist philosophy, found in *1,325 Buddhist Ways to Be Happy,* teach skillful living, which in turn leads to happy states of being.

Even the Dalai Lama tells us that you do not have to change your religion to benefit from the teachings of "The Happy One." This book allows readers of any faith, or none, to thoroughly explore the Buddha's ideas and to experience the truth of those ideas for themselves. The Dalai Lama's huge success with his book *The Art of Happiness* shows how spiritual seekers relate to the theme of appiness. If happiness is the purpose of life, then these sayings of the Buddha and of numerous Buddhist teachers and scholars show readers how to get there. The theme of *1,325 Buddhist Ways to Be Happy* crosses boundaries of cultural and belief traditions to help readers along in their journey on the path to happiness.

Being Compassionate

Compassion is the heartfelt wish that all beings could be free from suffering. Compassion and happiness are therefore inextricably linked. How can we be truly happy if we see others suffering? Cultivating a compassionate attitude toward others—helping them when we can, and not being upset when we cannot—helps create the positive karma for us to experience happiness, both now and in future lives.

Wisdom and compassion should dominate our thoughts, words, and actions.

When the heart is open, the sense of separateness diminishes considerably. This is an experience of seeing and knowing others to be not only part of you, but one with you.

See the need to calm your heart and your mind, and to find an inner balance. Reside with calm acceptance in the present without trying to fill it with anything.

For compassion to flourish in your heart, you must let go of discriminating between yourself and others, "me" and "them."

Sustain an optimistic, positive attitude.

Genuine compassion is based on the recognition that others have the right to happiness just as you do.

Compassion, loving-kindness, altruism, and a sense of brotherhood and sisterhood are the keys to human development, not only in the future but in the present as well.

DALAI LAMA

With a compassionate state of mind, your actions will always carry a tone of kindness and softness, which is useful in overcoming difficulty with anyone, child or adult.

As a Buddhist monk, my concern
extends to all members of the
human family and, indeed, to
all sentient beings who suffer.
I believe all suffering is caused
by ignorance. People inflict pain
on others in the selfish pursuit
of their own happiness
or satisfaction.
DALAI LAMA

Have a sense of gratitude to
everything, even difficult
emotions, because of their
potential in waking you up.

Silence is full of potential
wisdom.

Awakening compassion and
lessening selfishness are more
important than any other
spiritual practice.

Unconditionally accept what each moment has to offer.

Charles Dickens' *Christmas Carol* is a karmic tale. When Scrooge became more charitable and compassionate, he also became happier.

Be grateful to everyone.

Assume good intent.

Your patience will achieve more than your force.

Actions motivated only by genuine compassion create happiness.

When you smile a smile of compassion, you are encouraging your loving-kindness to wake up. You are encouraging yourself to be kind to yourself, because you are a thinking being.

Be spacious, full of loving-kindness, and compassionate— yet serene.

By changing our way of seeing things, we can reduce our current difficulties and avoid creating new ones.

Patience is motivated by our desire for inward and outward peace and by faith in our ability to accept things as they are.

It takes moment-to-moment patience to integrate our practice, to cultivate and nourish our heart and mind.

Compassion is based on others' fundamental rights to be happy and overcome suffering.

Train yourself to listen with compassion.

Compassion allows you to transform resentment into forgiveness and fear into respect.

We're simply getting smart about what brings suffering and what brings happiness. We're finally giving ourselves a break.

You are aiming for unshakable stability, an inability to be upset by any experience.

Acceptance is like a muscle that gets stronger the more you use it.

Find ways to bring a compassionate attitude to world affairs, to create a world in which everyone is considered equal and equally important.

Happiness and tolerance are strongly linked.

When you communicate with compassion, you are using language that does not have the elements of anger and irritation in it.

Through mindfulness, compassion, and kindness toward those who create suffering, you help generate conditions of happiness for those who cause harm.

Happiness arises from acceptance of yourself, others, the world, and this moment. Allow this moment to be as it is, and feel the peace that is always waiting for you.

One with compassion is kind even when angry; one without compassion will kill even as he smiles.
SHABKAR, TIBETAN POET

Simplicity, patience, compassion are your greatest treasures. Simple in actions and thoughts, you return to the source of being. Patient with both friends and enemies, you are in accord with the way things are. Compassionate toward yourself, you reconcile all beings in the world.
TAO TE CHING

With care and compassion, a warm heart and determination, difficult things can change and healthy, happy people can talk through their differences, reaching a compromise that all can live with.

No one can help us as much as our own compassionate thoughts.

If your heart can become loving and accepting, if you can cause your heart to have no anger, no resentment, then you have taken a great step on the Dharma path.

Not harming people or animals we do not like or feel indifferent to is a form of love and compassion that respects the wishes of others, who are simply trying to find happiness and avoid suffering.

The true practice is patience, not wanting anything special or unusual to happen.

Without holding or pushing away, without accepting or rejecting, you move along with daily work, doing what needs to be done, helping wherever you can.

Care, be compassionate, be present for others, listen, hear, and receive.

Compassion and appreciation grow from silence and sensitivity.

15

Say only what is true and useful.

If at any time something doesn't feel right to you, why not honor your feelings? An attitude of trusting yourself and your own basic wisdom and goodness is very important. The more you cultivate this trust in your own being, the easier you will find it will be to trust other people more and to see their basic goodness as well.

Learning to find refuge in calm and stillness allows waves of feeling to arise and then ebb away.

Recognize your capacity for being calm, for having under-standing, compassion, and peace. This is your true Buddha nature. Acknowledging this within you will help you suffer less. Bring your mind back to your Buddha nature, your good-ness and capacity for mindful-ness, calm, and seeing deeply.

The awakened mind is free-flowing, natural, well-rounded—like a mossy stone, nothing sticks to it.

In all activity, practice calmness.

Well-being, which is not sustainable, is not the same as happiness. Happiness is the ability to take all the insults of life as a vehicle for awakening—to enter into what the pioneer of stress-reduction, Jon Kabat-Zinn, has called the full catastrophe of our lives with an open mind and heart.

MARK EPSTEIN

Once you understand that the basic nature of humanity is compassionate rather than aggressive, your relationship to the world changes immediately. It helps you relax, trust, live at ease, be happier.

Acceptance and understanding of change is a deep spiritual insight that can transform our lives.

A moment of recognition about the judgmental mind is a moment of freedom and wisdom.

If you can accept anything and everything, you will be blissfully happy all the time.

The three greatest treasures are simplicity, patience, compassion.

One compassionate word, action, or thought can reduce another person's suffering and bring that person joy. One word can give comfort and confidence, destroy doubt, help someone avoid a mistake, reconcile a conflict, and open the door to liberation. One action can save a person's life or help the person take advantage of a rare opportunity. One thought can do the same, because thoughts always lead to words and actions. With compassion in our heart, every thought, word, and deed can bring a miracle.

The world spins without your help, people do what they do, and your life will run its course one way or the other. Sometimes your plans don't work out. You can decide not to get upset, anxious, or angry about things over which you have no power. You can choose to do your job and live your life with integrity, compassion, mindful observance, and a healthy sense of humor.

As long as space endures, and as long as sentient beings exist, may I, too, remain to dispel the misery of the world.
SHANTIDEVA

Compassion is based on knowing that all human beings have an innate desire to be happy and overcome suffering, just as you yourself do.

When you learn to appreciate a greater silence with yourself, your speech will begin to communicate calmness and clarity.

Be courageous—not locked into preconceptions of how things are, but courageous enough to be open and receptive to different possibilities.

A Zen-like concept is to walk a mile in another person's shoes. Whenever you catch yourself making "me" and "them" distinctions, spend a moment being the other person. Find yourself in him or her.
It may change your perspective and help you find tolerance, even compassion, toward someone you didn't understand.

The Buddha said that it is a great fortune to have an occupation that allows us to be happy, to help others, and to generate compassion and understanding in this world.

When you come to having a kind of honesty, gentleness, and good heartedness, combined with clarity about yourself, there's no obstacle to feeling loving-kindness for others, too.

The person who has no compassion in him or her can never be happy. The moment compassion is born in you, you feel better.

If your heart is large and you have understanding and compassion, a word or deed will not have the power to make you suffer. It depends on your way of receiving, embracing, and transforming.

Rediscover the power of self-forgiveness.

When you are guided by compassion and loving-kindness, you are able to look deeply into the heart of reality and see the truth.

Nurturing calmness, understanding, and trust within ourselves impacts directly on our way of seeing each person and entering our lives.

We burden ourselves by thinking that happiness consists of having certain things or acting in a certain way. When we leave aside our limited views, it is possible to open up to deeper experiences of joy.

When we realize in our own experience that happiness comes not from reaching out but from letting go, not from seeking pleasurable experience but from opening to the moment to what is true, a transformation of energy frees the compassion within us. Our minds are no long bound up in pushing away pain or holding on to pleasure. Compassion is the natural response of an open heart. When we settle back and open to what's happening in each moment, without attachment or aversion, we are experience itself. From this attitude that we develop in our practice, we can begin to manifest true compassionate action in the world.

Compassion is the source of
nonviolent action,
and it brings us inner strength
and mental peace.
These qualities also bring us
more smiles, friendship, and
harmony.
So compassion is really
something very precious.
DALAI LAMA

All beings wish for happiness,
so extend your compassion to
everyone.

Partake of each meal with
gratitude.

When we open and note
just what's happening in each
moment, without holding on,
without pushing away, without
struggle, then we fine an inner
rhythm—this brings a certain
ease and effortlessness to
practice.

Being Kind

The Dalai Lama says that his religion is kindness. Kindness breeds kindness. If you are compassionate to yourself, you are likely to act with kindness toward others. You can make kindness the basis of your spiritual practice and by doing so can contribute compassion, serenity, and happiness to the complex world.

No one who has been generous
has ever perished in destitution.
IBN' ARABI

Does happiness make us kind, or
does being kind make us happy?
MATTHIEU RICARD

The happiest man is he who has
no trace of malice in his soul.
PLATO

Everyone can learn from your
kindness, and everyone deserves
your kindness.

Act in a wholesome way and you
will be happy.

Patience is the foundation
of discovering simplicity.
Patience is a gesture
of profound kindness.

Grow in charity and generosity
and humility.

Develop generosity
at whatever level you find it
arising in your heart.

Instead of reacting to emotions, just observe them with kindness and patience.

The best we can do is to help when we can, to witness each other with kindness, to offer our presence, to show trust in life.

Be kind, unconditionally kind, on this breath alone. Forget about the future. On only this breath, no matter what the circumstances, just be kind in whatever way is appropriate.

Cultivating warmth, fearlessness, and acceptance of both others and *ourselves*, we become more friendly, forgiving, and happy.

28

Repressing anger is not healthy. The best antidote to anger is loving-kindness, to yourself and whoever made you angry. Loving-kindness develops from realizing that only someone who is unhappy will hurt someone else. Therefore, the person who hurt us cannot be happy, and we should try to feel compassion rather than anger toward them.

Loving-kindness motivates you to behave kindly to all beings at all times and to speak gently both in their presence and in their absence.

Any gesture of kindness, any gesture of honesty and seeing clearly, will affect how you experience your world. What you do for yourself, you also do for others; and what you do for others, you do for yourself.

If we remain open to experience and change, we find ourselves able to deal with life's different weathers.

Only by being fully present and cultivating gratitude, generosity, and kindness can we find the renewable source of happiness in ourselves in each moment.

Let your kindness rain on all.

If a man speaks or acts with pure thought, happiness follows him like a shadow that never leaves him.
BUDDHA

Through kindness, the world softens. Be kind to all beings and things.

Those with an open heart in all things will find great happiness.

There is no greater happiness than when your heart becomes pure and simple, like that of a child.

Loving-kindness as a divine abode is often described as the sun whose rays shine indiscriminately on the whole Earth and all living things.

When you become calm and serene on the inside, the world becomes more calm and serene on the outside.

Repay the kindness
that you have received.

Desire little, be content,
and repay acts of kindness.

Smile at both the flower
and the garbage in you,
and you will embrace both.

Filter your questions.

Eleven benefits of loving-kindness: the first three are going to sleep happily, dreaming no evil dreams, waking happily. You will be dear to human beings, dear to nonhuman beings, immune from poison; deities will protect you; you will have quick mental concentration; your facial expression will be beautified; you will have a peaceful death; and then you will be born into the blissful realm, or brahma realm.

For each thought and feeling that comes up, you could ask, "Does this create well-being or does it create suffering?"

The best way is to understand yourself, and then you will understand everything.
SHUNRYN SUZUKI

Thousands of candles can be lighted from a single candle, and the life of the candle will not be shortened. Happiness never decreases by being shared.
BUDDHA

Happiness is not about what happens to you, but how you choose to respond to what happens.

The simple person does not take himself too seriously or too tragically. He goes on his merry way, his heart light. The simple person has no secrets, and he acts without guile, ulterior motives, agendas, or plans.
ANDRÉ COMTE-SPONVILLE

Let your kind words diffuse someone else's unhappiness.

Go to the other shore— the shore of non-anger, peace, and liberation.

When we really let go, we become and identify with everything.

Speak kind words, words rejoiced at and welcomed, words that bear ill will to none; always speak kindly to others.
SUTTA NIPATA

We can protect life, practice generosity, behave responsibly, and consume mindfully.

Lasting happiness comes from deep kindness and respect for all beings and all life. Clear wisdom sees what is skillful, appropriate, timely, and true.

What is important is the way we respond to whatever happens, because this will shape our future.

If you consistently cultivate generosity and loving-kindness to all, you'll make lots of friends, many will love you, and you'll feel relaxed and peaceful.

Practice *metta* (loving-kindness) by saying: "May I be filled with loving-kindness. May I be well. May I be peaceful and at ease. May I be happy." Repeat for others you know.

Offer kindness to those who are undeserving of it.

Be kind even to those you do not love. Be grateful to them for giving you the opportunity to do a kindness.

Do you really want to be happy? Just pay attention and be kind, unconditionally kind, on this breath alone. No matter what the circumstances, just be kind. Everything else will work itself out.

A generous heart, kind speech, and a life of service and compassion are the things that renew humanity.

Let go of even the most subtle expectations, and learn to respond to situations with a caring heart.

One well-chosen word that brings the listener peace is better than a thousand words spoken in vain.

Your attachments give you the opportunity to develop patience and kindness toward them, so the grasping will melt away.

Make kindness your religion.

Start the day be reaffirming your intention to practice loving-kindness and compassion. Remind yourself to work at letting go of ego-clinging, selfishness, possessiveness, aggression, resentment, confusion.

In every situation, resting in openness and acting with kindness are the right answer.

You have it easily in your power to increase the sum total of this world's happiness now. How? By giving a few words of sincere appreciation to someone who is lonely or is discouraged. Perhaps you will forget tomorrow the kind words you say today, but the recipient may cherish them over a lifetime.

DALE CARNEGIE

If you are awake and honest, you will act from kindness of heart.

Happy people like themselves.

When you practice loving-kindness, your voice will become sweet and soft.

It is an act of great kindness to learn how to let go in this life, to be with what is, to harmonize yourself with life's changes, and to be open to the mystery of the unknown.

The Buddha encouraged useful speech—a request for "deep" speech—about important topics that we care about, rather than anything that pops into your mind.

When you clearly understand which of your actions will cause an effect of happiness, and which actions cause suffering, then you know how to find happiness and avoid suffering.

One of the many rewards of acting with kindness is that it helps keep life simple.

Smile a little.

You are already complete, whole, perfect. All this action and effort to become special is only making you very unspecial and creating tremendous pain and suffering.

What you do for yourself— any gesture of kindness, any gesture of gentleness or honesty toward yourself—is something you are also doing for others.

Equanimity is happiness surpassing the body. So we use the words *serene* and *drifting* to describe that happiness. Joy and happiness relate somewhat to the body, and thus they are somewhat impermanent. Equanimity is permanent.
TIEN CONG TRAN

Your willingness to be kind and compassionate toward yourself is the foundation for inner peace and peace for the planet.

If you know anything that is helpful and true, find the right time. Desist from impetuous speech. Think about it first, make sure that it will be helpful and that it's also true and the right time has come. The right time has come when the other person is agreeable to listening and in a peaceful frame of mind. It should be at a time when you have loving feelings for the other person. Use this whenever you want to tell others what they should and shouldn't do.

Practice *metta* (loving-kindness) by saying: "May I be free from danger. May I have mental happiness. May I have physical happiness. May I have ease of well-being." Repeat these phrases for others you know.

Anyone who is truly kind can never be unhappy.
CONFUCIUS

Speak gently to everyone and they will respond accordingly.

We need to accept fear and anger with a genuine loving-kindness for ourselves, and then let them go. If you suppress them, the attachment nurtures their roots. It is all right to let it come and let it go.

Reflect on the kindness of everyone you meet.

Try to smile at the people you see, or at least look at them directly and acknowledge them as fellow human beings.

Rather than gossiping about others and saying unpleasant things about them, it is important to think of others kindly and always wish for their well-being and happiness. If you cannot find something nice to say about someone, it is always best to say nothing at all.

Loving-kindness has the capacity to soften the hardness and release the contraction of aversion.

The space created when we let go of our attachments brings a heart vast in its kindness.

45

Say little. But when you speak, utter gentle words that touch the heart. Be truthful. Express kindness.

In moments when you cultivate stillness, you are offering a great gift of kindness to yourself.

Serenity and calm develop as we learn to accept imperfection in others as well as in ourselves.

When your actions are motivated by generosity, love, or wisdom, the results are happiness and peace.

Finding Peace

Peace begins with us. You are not powerless on this planet; you can embrace a spiritual path that brings tranquility to your heart and mind, which is the first step toward bringing peace to the world. Cultivated inner calmness will beget gentle speech and moral actions, such as gentle caring for others. When you bring the qualities of peace to your communications, you will radiate peace out into the world.

Practice letting go,
and you cultivate inner peace.
Practice fully experiencing what
is happening in each moment
with as much awareness as
possible, not wanting it to be
different than it is.

Let go of winning and losing,
find joy.

Without our personal prejudices
and attachments, we develop a
natural friendliness and
contentment toward all our
experiences and for all beings.

The man who in his work finds
silence, and who sees that
silence is work, this man in truth
sees the light and in all his works
finds peace.

Go into the sunshine and be happy with what you see.

There's a sense of well-being that comes from being totally independent, from not needing other things. If we are constantly giving in to our impulse to do this or take that, we will never know what well-being is.

Letting go a little improves life. Letting go a lot brings happiness and joy.

Happiness resides not in possessions nor in gold, for the feeling of happiness dwells in the soul.
DEMOCRITUS

On the edge of the forest, live joyfully, without desire.
BUDDHA

If you eat or drink something that is healthy and nourishing, your feeling of happiness will grow as you become aware of it.

Here it is—right now. Start thinking about it and you'll miss it.

Many people look for happiness outside themselves, but true happiness must come from inside us.

With a peaceful heart,
whatever happens can be met
with wisdom.

Every waking second
is a chance to look past who you
think you are right through
to who you truly are.

Once you are able to locate
peace and love in yourself,
you will have greater ease
locating it in other people.

Hope is itself a species
of happiness and, perhaps,
the chief happiness
which this world affords.
SAMUEL JOHNSON

Become more centered, balanced, straightforward, calm, and clear amid temporary weather conditions.

Free yourself by using this constant reminder—
"It's not important.
I don't have to...."

To be frugal means to have a high joy-to-stuff ratio. If you get 1 unit of joy for each material possession, that's frugal. But if you need 10 possessions to even begin registering on the joy meter, you're missing the point of being alive.

The Buddha pointed us toward three skillful thoughts: letting go, or generosity in the highest sense; loving-kindness/friendliness; and compassion.

Moments of stillness and genuine simplicity offer glimpses
of what it means to live in a spiritual and free way.
We know we do not need yet more sounds, thoughts,
experiences, possessions, or attainments. We have had so many,
yet they have failed to quench our thirst for freedom and stillness.
The clutter of our lives and minds entangles us in an escalating cycle
of alienation, haste, and exhaustion.

The greatest part of our happiness or misery depends
on our dispositions and not on our circumstances.
MARTHA WASHINGTON

Never continue in a job you don't enjoy. If you're happy in what you're doing, you'll like yourself, you'll have inner peace. And if you have that, along with physical health, you will have had more success than you could possibly have imagined.
JOHNNY CARSON

Be true to yourself—
if something makes you
unhappy, try something else.

Dare to be naive.
BUCKMINSTER FULLER

There is relief in finally dropping and getting rid of excess baggage through development of an inner certainty about the illusory nature of things.

If you let go a little,
you will have a little peace;
if you let go a lot,
you will have even more peace.

Live sanely and gracefully,
impeccably, and without regret.

If you do not get it from yourself,
where will you go for it?
ALAN WATTS

Lighten up—and find joy in
whatever needs to be done.

Begin and end each day
with a moment of stillness.

Find out who and what you are,
then you can reside in
everlasting bliss as long
as you choose—both in this
body and out of it.

Make it a point to be happy to be
here. The first thought of the day
should be positive and special.

It is not how much we have,
but how much we enjoy,
that makes happiness.

Celebrate your happiness by never questioning it.

Appreciate each moment as a vehicle for developing wisdom.

To have peace, we must first have understanding. Understanding is not possible without gentle, loving communication.

Happiness cannot be found through great effort and willpower. It is already present, in open relaxation and letting go.

No matter what you have done, said, thought, or accomplished, you have a capacity inside you for transformation, and it can bring lasting happiness.

Tranquility comes when we let go of the urge to control everything and instead relate to each moment with openness and awareness.

We live our lives waiting for the weekend, a vacation, some new object to own, waiting with desire for some new happiness always just out of reach.

If, by renouncing a lesser happiness, one may realize a greater happiness, let the wise man renounce the lesser, having regard for the greater happiness.
TIEN CONG TRAN

Your awareness of the present
is the nourishment
you have been looking for.

Tranquility is achieved when you
are in harmony with all beings
and all situations, knowing that
everything is precisely the way it
is meant to be.

When wishes are few,
the heart is happy.

The fact that you are fresh and
pleasant to be around already
changes a great deal.

I seek to take as my essential practice the yoga of exchanging self with others.
SHANTIDEVA

Whatever the day's weather, we have to accept it.
To complain about the rain, or lack of it, shows a mind out of tune with nature.

If you want to be happy, be.
HENRY DAVID THOREAU

Go straight to happiness and fulfillment, and skip the intermediary of desire.
Just try it in this moment.
Let go and see what happens.

Inner peace is possible anywhere and in any situation. It is within you. You are just as likely to reach full enlightenment in your current situation as the Buddha was in his—if you make it your first priority.

In renunciation lies a delicious taste of simplicity and peace. Hope for little and have nothing to lose.

Let go and get used to letting go—to experience more inner peace.

Dance with life—don't try to control it or figure it out.

61

The option to be happy
is just as much a possibility
as the option to suffer.

Happy cooks make happy food.

Your treasure house is in
yourself. It contains all you
will ever need.

Take away your opinions and
what is left? Take away your
opinion of your condition
and situation, and your mind is
clear like space—and you
will see clearly, hear clearly,
smell clearly.

What ripens in any moment
are seeds sown in the past.
In this moment, choose
consciously to sow seeds
for happiness and health.
Breathe your awareness
into this moment.

Happiness is not complicated.
In fact, it is the simplest thing
in the world.

Gently let go of everything—not
through force, not by slaying it,
but simply by seeing the passing
show as process and flow.

Sukha is the state of lasting well-
being that manifests itself when
we have freed ourselves of
mental blindness and afflictive
emotions. It is also the wisdom
that allows us to see the world as
it is, without veils or distortions.
It is, finally, the joy of moving
toward inner freedom as well as
the loving-kindness that radiates
toward others.

When there is no grasping, there's a spacious feeling of acceptance with the way things are—offering the nourishment you've been looking for.

From a peaceful center, we can respond instead of react.

See things as they are, observe, let everything go as it passes.

Affirmation: *I rest in tranquility and grace. I am calm, fulfilled, and happy. I take refuge in my calm center.*

Happiness does not come from any kind of acquisitiveness, whether material or psychological. Happiness comes from letting go.

Our smiling, breathing, and being peace can make peace.

As you walk, you may see, hear, or smell something that you want to savor. Enjoy what you encounter, and breathe to be fully present.

Don't believe everything you think.

Peace and happiness are always available and are with you at every instant.

An attack on your way of thinking is just an attack on a thought, not on you. If you can see it as such and if you can say, *Okay, that is just a thought,* you are one step closer to liberation. Contemplate the positive qualities of the object or experience.

Think of all the beauty still left around you and be happy.
ANNE FRANK

Joy is not in things; it is in us.

Suffering is actually essential to happiness. You have to know being too cold to appreciate being warm.

Human happiness and human satisfaction must ultimately come from within oneself.
DALAI LAMA

Your experience will be the most blissful if you can live in the simple awareness that you are—that you exist, you are aware, without marrying your essence to mundane identifications like your shape and size.

If you observe a truly happy man, you will find that he is happy in the course of living life twenty-four crowded hours each day.

67

Carefully review your current life: your schedule, finances, work, relationships, family life, home, leisure activities, possessions, goals, and spiritual life. Ask yourself, for each area: *What would it be like to greatly simplify this area? If it became simpler, would I feel happier?* Begin the process of mindful change.

Happiness can only be felt if you do not set any conditions.

If a person is genuinely interested in achieving happiness, then that person does not need sophisticated machines or material wealth.

As soon as we become mindful, paying attention to what's happening, seeing how everything is arising and passing away, then the grasping and greed decreases. There's nothing to hold onto. It's all bubbles.

Seek happiness in the present,
and you'll find it in the future.

You do not need to cover up
your perfect, inherent beauty
with identity after identity.
You need nothing more than
what you have. You are as
complete as you will ever be.
You are complete as you are.

What you are looking for
is what is looking.
SAINT FRANCIS OF ASSISI

Wherever you are is the perfect
place to rest in openness.

The wisdom of the heart is here, now, at any moment. It has always been here, and it is never too late to find it. The wholeness and freedom we seek is our own true nature, who we really are. Whenever we start a spiritual practice, read a spiritual book, or contemplate what it means to live well, we have begun to open to this truth.

Peace is most often found in the absence of prejudice, resistance, and judgment.

You feel pleasure because a desire is gone, for the moment. You feel pleasure because there is no desire, no tension, no future, no past, and no unnecessary mind activity. Pleasure is a taste of freedom. This spaciousness allows pleasure to dominate your awareness.

It becomes a way of life to stay awake, slow down, and notice.

Have room for everything
and hold on to nothing.

You only need what will make
your life better and happier, not
what will weigh it down.

No one can escape death
and unhappiness. If people
expect only happiness in life,
they will be disappointed.
BUDDHA

Try not to take yourself
so seriously.

Do not be dependent on external circumstances for happiness.

It is a radical simplicity to affirm that our happiness cannot be purchased.

Practice contentment— find happiness with what you have and with who you are.

Accept what you cannot change.

Genuine happiness and peace lie
in contentment and simplicity.
You don't need very much
to be happy.

Be wise, disciplined,
and nonviolent
and you will find peace.

Happiness comes from within.
If you choose to be happy,
no one and no thing can take
the feeling from you.

Happiness is a state of activity.
ARISTOTLE

Happiness is never stopping to think whether you are.

The key is to wake up, become more alert.

At the center of your being you have the answer, you know who you are, and you know what you want.

LAO-TZU

The more a man finds his sources of pleasure in himself, the happier he will be.... The highest, most varied and lasting pleasures are those of the mind.

ARTHUR SCHOPENHAUER

Success is not found in what
you have achieved, but rather
in who you have become.

Be precisely where you are,
who you are,
what you are.

When desire ends,
there is peace.

Laugh more.
When you laugh,
compulsive thought disappears
and you are completely
in the present moment.

The stop sign reminds us
to slow our pace,
take a moment's rest,
and look around.

Leave your life alone
and just live.

Speak words that create peace,
are pleasant to hear, and are
spoken at the proper time. Speak
only what is true and useful.

Be happy where you are. Learn
that locked within the moments
of each day are all the joys and
peace we want. The meaning lies
in the moment.

Renunciation is not about depriving ourselves
of that which brings us joy and happiness—that would be absurd;
it is about abandoning what causes us inexhaustible and relentless
distress. It is about having the courage to rid ourselves of dependency
on the root causes of suffering.... It comes down to asking ourselves,
with respect to certain aspects of our lives: Is this going to make me
happier? Genuine happiness—as opposed to contrived euphoria—
endures through life's ups and downs.

The wise man has nothing left to expect or to hope for. Because he is
entirely happy, he needs nothing. Because he needs nothing, he is
entirely happy.
ANDRE COMTE-SPONVILLE

It is a sane decision to renounce mental poisons. Stop the game of alternating between happiness and suffering.

It's all funny.

Recognizing the emotion at the very moment it forms; understanding that it is but a thought, devoid of intrinsic existence; and allowing it to dissipate spontaneously so as to avoid the chain reaction it would normally unleash—all these are at the heart of Buddhist contemplative practice.

Even when it rains, the sunshine is always there a little bit above the clouds.

What makes you happy will most likely also be a worthwhile contribution to the world.

True peace is not a destination projected into the future, but a path and practice of the moment.

Once you realize and experience that you cannot figure out the mysteries of life and its play of events, it will be easier to open yourself to a whole new way of experiencing what is. Pure awareness is a way of perceiving that does not involve the mind or thoughts. To exist as pure awareness is to exist simply as your essence.

It is through this perception that you may eventually gain insight into what you truly are, what life is, and what the universe is all about.

Each moment you are alive is unique. Appreciate and make the most of it.

Be just plain happy. Be happy in the being and the knowing.

Being centered in the face of the pull of the outer world, not having to look elsewhere for something to fill us up or make us happy, we can be at home wherever we find ourselves.

All that you need to be really happy is something to be enthusiastic about.

Happy is the house
where a man awakes.

The path begins when you find
what is sacred to you,
on an everyday level.

Freedom and happiness
are found in flexibility and
the ease with which you deal
with change.

Happiness is in the heart,
not in the circumstances.

One day, some people came to the master and asked:
How can you be so happy in a world of such impermanence,
where you cannot protect your loved ones from harm, illness, and death?
The master held up a glass and said: *Someone gave me this glass, and I*
really like this glass. It holds my water admirably and it glistens in the sunlight.
One day the wind may blow it off the shelf, or my elbow may knock it
from the table. I know this glass is already broken, so I enjoy it incredibly.
ACHAAN CHAH

The first kind of happiness is the one that's most familiar to us—
the happiness of sense pleasures. This is the kind of happiness
we experience from being in pleasant surroundings, having good
friends, enjoying beautiful sights and sounds and delicious tastes and
smells, and having agreeable sensations in the body. Even though these
pleasures are impermanent and fleeting, in the moments we're
experiencing them, they bring us a certain delight.
JOSEPH GOLDSTEIN

Appreciate happy unplanned
moments.

Very little is needed
to make a happy life.
It is all within yourself.
MARCUS AURELIUS

Appreciate the happiness
of heading home.

Find things to be happy about
on your own.

To create peace in the world,
you must be unruffled within.
Walk in stillness, act in harmony.
The serenity that emanates
from you will create peace.

Wisdom replaces ignorance
when we realize that happiness
does not lie in the accumulation
of more and more pleasant
feelings.

Tranquility is fostered by time
alone and time in nature.

A supple mind helps you
reconcile the external changes
going on around you.

As you walk and eat, be where you are—or you'll miss your life.

In work, do what you enjoy.

Happiness is not having what you want, it's wanting what you have.

Set an alcohol-free happy hour for yourself each day.

We can be happy
without having a reason.

Feel deserving of happiness.

Happiness comes in relaxed
simplicity, living in present
awareness, and contentment
with this life that is granted
to you.

Keep as many of your options
open as possible.

The secret of Happiness is Freedom, and the secret of Freedom, Courage.
THUCYDIDES

There are lots of ways of being miserable, but there's only one way of being comfortable, and that is to stop running round after happiness. If you make up your mind not to be happy there's no reason why you shouldn't have a fairly good time.
EDITH WHARTON

Everything invites you to cherish it.

Imagine yourself to be as happy as possible. Your ability to imagine this will be proof of this dormant capacity. Within a week, you will start feeling that you are becoming very happy for no reason at all.

With sustained effort
and sincerity, discipline and
self-control, the wise become
like islands.

Behold the jewel in the lotus,
the enlightened mind
that grows in the center
of human consciousness.

The release from stress, not to
mention stillness, inner peace,
nirvana—these are already
inside us. We don't need to
search for them elsewhere.
We just need to sit and look.

When you tune in to the very
essence of what you are, you will
find silence and every answer to
every question ever posed.

Look into your situation and see how rich you are inside. What you have in the present moment is a gift. Begin to practice being in the present moment right away. The moment you begin to practice, you'll feel happy right away.

Why rush through some moments to get to other, better ones? We don't have to fill up our moments with activity and more thinking in order for them to be rich—quite the opposite is true. Be completely open to each moment, accepting it in its fullness, knowing that, like the butterfly from the cocoon, things unfold in their own time.

The walls around your true self must be penetrated, the many layers of the onion have to be peeled away, to reach that beautiful, perfect center of pure peace and energy.

Develop the capacity to be happy in any surroundings.

Happiness cannot come from without. It must come from within. It is not what we see and touch or that which others do for us which makes us happy; it is that which we think and feel and do, first for the other fellow and then for ourselves.

HELEN KELLER

Wisdom is shown by radiating an inner peace—and joy, warmth, kindness, connectedness, integrity, love.

Experience all things with the enthusiasm of a child, as if you were seeing it for the first time.

Contemplate the way in which life depends on variety—and resolve not to let others' differences disturb your tranquility.

Peace is in the doing.
It is not being locked inside a
quiet room. Move the anxiety
you attach to an activity out of
the way. You have to have your
stillness and keep moving, too.

There is no fire like passion,
no scourge like hatred,
no ache like hunger, no suffering
greater than mental anguish,
no happiness greater than peace.

Asking yourself *What am I doing?*
will help you overcome the habit
of wanting to complete things
quickly. Smile to yourself and
say, *Washing this dish is the most
important job in my life.* If your
thoughts are carrying you away,
you need mindfulness to
intervene.

Make happiness a priority.

Repeat: *May I be happy just as I am, May I be peaceful with whatever is happening.*

Be happy with the way you look.

Try to find the blessing of inner silence and peace, and mindfully speak to and listen for interconnectedness between yourself and others.

Make yourself an island that the flood cannot overwhelm.

Streamlining and downsizing can help us find peace.

Every day is a good day.

Spend a whole day in bed to rest, or a whole day out of doors. All that matters is that you have a chance to shut out the world and cocoon for a while.

Peace of mind produces right values, right values produce right thoughts, right thoughts produce right actions.

The quieter you become, the
more you can hear.
RAM DASS

Rejoice in whatever life gives
you. Do not crave otherwise.
Know that whatever you have
been given is for your own
highest good.

It is not doing the thing we
like to do, but liking the thing
we have to do, that makes
life blessed.
GOETHE

True happiness leads to
tranquility. As the mind calms
down, it naturally becomes
more concentrated. As your
concentration deepens, you can
proceed to train the mind
toward full concentration.

You have the capacity to live in a way that the next twenty-four hours will bring peace, joy, and happiness to yourself and others.

Believe in the possibility of happiness.

In the morning when you wake up, aspire to keep a wide-open heart and mind.

Make your world your monastery—wherever you are, whatever you encounter is meant to provide you with exactly what you need to work with right now.

When you learn to stop obsessing, to stop chewing on the same old ideas and emotions over and over again, that is when you find some peace. The idea is not to stop thinking permanently. The idea is to be able to have a choice: Do you feel like thinking right now or not? Will thinking help you recognize the perfection of the present moment? Is this thought something you want on your mind right now or not? Is life slipping by while you are caught up in thoughts of the future and past? Thinking is an addiction. When it becomes your choice, to think or not to think—that is freedom.

The happiest people are those who think the most interesting thoughts. Those who decide to use leisure as a means of mental development, who love good music, good books, good pictures, good company, good conversation, are the happiest people in the world. And they are not only happy in themselves, they are the cause of happiness in others.

Learn to simplify, strip away your expectations and desires, let go of your fears and projections, and see the simple truth of each moment. Understanding and wise responsiveness manifest in your speech, actions, and choices.

It is rare that happiness alights just so on the desire that called for it.
MARCEL PROUST

Awareness will take you where you need to go.

There is a sense of freedom when we accept that we're not in control.

Each day, accept everything that comes to you as a gift! At night, mentally give it all back. You become free—as no one can take anything from you, for nothing is yours.

Each moment, you can live fully. Is there any moment that would not be richer if you were fully awake?

Realize that being who you want to be, and doing what you want to do, is self-respect.

Every man wants to be happy, but in order to be so he needs first to understand what happiness is.
JEAN-JACQUES ROUSSEAU

Contentment comes from
neither doing nor having,
but from being.

Be here now! It is important
to live life in the moment as it
unfolds and to experience
happiness here and now,
rather than to be distracted
by memories of happiness
or future possibilities.

The best thing to do is to try to
be as much at peace with the
world as you can.

Those who are awake live in a
state of constant amazement.

99

Set aside a place in which
to be happy alone.

Be determined to live
a happy life.

To embrace a true Zen state,
we need to stop desiring these
things (any thing) and simply
step into them. That includes
desire for release from stress,
desire for stillness, desire
for inner peace—
they are still desires.

We often find ourselves taking
refuge in other things that we
think are going to bring us
happiness. They are not bad
things, but they do not bring
lasting happiness.
A lasting happiness is one
that illuminates our being.

Happiness is simply happiness.
You are transported. You are no
longer part of the world that the
human mind creates. You are
no longer part of the past.
You are no longer part of time
at all. When you are really happy,
time disappears.

Make the most of yourself,
for that is all there is to you.
RALPH WALDO EMERSON

Open to seeing things as they are
without adding anything extra.

You are full of opinions
and preconceptions.
To find happiness,
you must lose them.

Be happily alone in a crowd.

It would be easier not to go to all the trouble of constantly ruminating over our suffering. It would be better just to think about something else, go to the beach, and have a nice cold beer!
DALAI LAMA

Recognize and honor your happy self and inner spirit.

Right here is paradise, nirvana.

Only you can make you happy.

Simplicity brings more happiness than complexity.

Be satisfied with what you have.

The combination of effort, inner detachment, and genuine equanimity helps us come home within ourselves—and find inner peace.

Learning to let go is the key
to happiness.

Magical things happen every day,
if we allow it. Think of daylight,
of the stars at night, a flower.
A dandelion is a miracle.

If you are not a happy person
inside, then nothing outside you
will ever make you happy and
able to feel love.

Read slowly and calmly so that
the very act of reading is peace.

Do not inquire why or whither,
but just enjoy your ice cream
while it's on your plate.

Hear all sounds as
beautiful music.

Do the one thing that really
makes you happy
when you are very sad.

The present is the only time
that any of us has. Moment-to-
moment awareness makes our
experiences more vivid and our
lives more real.

If you are faced with a feeling of confusion or stagnation, take an hour, an afternoon, or several days to reflect on what it is that will truly bring you happiness.

Becoming curious about how we suffer does not mean that we can no longer enjoy eating ice cream. But once we begin to understand the confusion of the untrained mind, we won't look to ice cream and say, *That's happiness*. We will realize that the mind can be happy devoid of ice cream. We will realize that the mind is content and happy by nature.

Expecting happiness from an identity you have purchased is delusional. The same is true when you think the role of mother, father, president, or millionaire will make you totally happy. In and of itself, an identification won't make you happy.

Have gratitude, even for difficult emotions, because of their potential to wake you up.

If you bank on achieving genuine happiness and fulfillment by finding the perfect mate, getting a great car, having a big house, the best insurance, a fine reputation, the top job—if these are your focus, wish also for good luck in life's lottery.

B. ALAN WALLACE

Each moment is like a snowflake—unique, unspoiled, unrepeatable—and can be appreciated in its surprisingness.

If a man who has just moved into a luxury apartment on the hundredth floor of a brand-new building is deeply unhappy, the only thing he'll look for is a window to jump out of.

DALAI LAMA

Remember that no matter where you are or what you face, within your heart peace is possible.

Be glad of life because it gives you the chance to love and to work and to play and to look up at the stars.

You have to believe that inner peace is possible, that you are already perfect, that you don't need to add anything to yourself. It requires a leap of faith.

Feel supremely happy.

I have come to see that our problem is that we don't know what happiness is. We confuse it with a life uncluttered by feelings of anxiety, rage, doubt, and sadness. But happiness is something entirely different. It's the ability to receive the pleasant without grasping and the unpleasant without condemning.

MARK EPSTEIN

By letting go of all we believe we are, by letting go of thinking we're the body or the mind, that we're brilliant or stupid, and so on, we become whole and awaken. If we let go of everything, we can have anything. If we hold anything at all, we lose everything else and that thing we cling to changes and becomes a cause for pain.

Enlightenment is uninterrupted happiness, awareness of the source of all and everything, and conscious oneness with the all and everything.

Pause between swallowing one bite of food and picking up the next one.

Truly happy people are fully present in the moment.

Whether we regard our situation as heaven or hell depends on our perception.
PEMA CHODRON

Start rearranging priorities rather than taking life for granted. Learn to find joy in everything you do and in every interpersonal contact.

Understanding Good Karma

Everyone wants to be happy and to avoid suffering and dissatisfaction. This is a universal truth that does not depend on any personal factor. An understanding of karma can be greatly beneficial. Karma is the law of cause and effect. When you clearly understand which of your actions will cause happiness and which will cause suffering, then you know how to find happiness and avoid suffering. If we engage in positive, skillful actions (which are the cause of happiness), we will definitely experience their result, which is happiness.

You get what you give; what goes around comes around. Call it *karma,* or simply reaping what you sow.

Recognize the positive seeds, touch them, and help them manifest on the upper level or our consciousness.

Reflecting on the law of karma brings an appreciation of the preciousness of our life and a sense not to squander the rare opportunity we have.

All your happiness and all your suffering are created by you, by your own mind and motivation.

If you keep your situation happy day by day, you will eventually reach the greatest happiness of enlightenment.

Abandon minds of anger and unhappiness, and wherever you go be happy.

We get so accustomed to certain habits that even when we're given the opportunity to change, we don't take it. We get comfortable with being angry and unhappy.

There is only one minute in which you are alive: this minute, here and now. The only way to live is by accepting each minute as an unrepeatable miracle.

Once the profound nature of
karma is properly understood,
a path that can lead to a happier
life may be discovered.

Reflect on what is truly of value,
what gives meaning to life.
Set your priorities on that basis.

Live fully, in each moment.
Focus your effort on the present
instead of insisting on when the
future must be.

Cherish the blessings
that appear in your life.

Make the decision to be happy and content.

Have the courage to let a thought slip by and not chase after it.

Happiness is not a station you arrive at, but a manner of traveling.

A rare person sees how far there is to go but remains unhurried, carefully placing each foot on the ground, delighting in the views and sounds but never getting lost. Their journey is completed in every step.

It takes but a split second to check whether your action or words
will produce happiness or suffering, so doing so is definitely
a worthwhile habit to develop. Also, the art of listening to others
helps us realize we do not need to say everything that comes
into our minds. And when someone shouts at you,
you are under no obligation to shout back!

Whichever seeds we water will blossom and grow into plants.
If we repeatedly act out of anger, we are watering the seeds of anger.
If we meet our anger with kindness, then the anger seeds cannot grow,
but a loving plant will come in its place.

Our attitude is the problem.
Happiness is possible only when
what we call *suffering* no longer
causes us distress.

Be willing to be present
with whatever arises,
no matter what it is.

Take time to play.

Your actions will bear fruit
when the time is ripe.

117

Cultivate peace of mind
which does not separate one's
self from one's surroundings.
When that is done successfully,
then everything else
follows naturally.
ROBERT M. PIRSIG

Dream as if you'll dream forever.
Live as if you'll die today.

Live joyfully, without desire.

Happiness depends on ourselves.
ARISTOTLE

At the end of the day, before going to sleep, rejoice in any fulfilled aspirations.

You can break the pattern, change the next moment, do something different—something enlightened, creative, imaginative, compassionate, wise, fresh.

There are three doors—thought, speech, and actions—with which karma is made. If an unskillful thought arises, be careful that it does not turn into speech or action.

Cultivate self-knowledge.

Believe in what makes you feel good. Believe in what makes you happy.

Seek to be balanced, centered, and simple in the midst of change.

Consider careful and wise choices.

Understand the happiness of nongrasping.

The understanding of how things are happening becomes the gateway to the highest kind of happiness.

Unless you see clearly that changing something will further the cause of happiness, then it should be left alone.

If we are not angry,
we live in peace and happiness.
If we are not hostile,
we live in peace and happiness.
That is nirvana.

Actions that are kind, unselfish, and virtuous help others; help you accumulate good karma; and are an expression of wisdom, higher sanity, and enlightenment.

121

Become more yielding, more equanimous, more flexible—giving up rigid stances and fixed ideas.

It is how we respond to something that will create what comes into our karmic path in the future.

Awareness is the key that unlocks the door of the present moment. Wake up to this present moment.

Suffering can be eliminated by eliminating desire. Let go of the stuff. Let go of the grasping and the wanting and the absolutely-have-to-having, and you'll feel an amazing, uplifting sense of freedom.

According to feng shui,
red carpet in the bedroom brings
good fortune and happiness.

Transforming attachment
into generosity reduces negative
karma and leads to the causes
of happiness.

Remember that understanding
karma is an important key to
understanding happiness.

Seize it all.
What you seize is what you get.

If we plant peaches,
we will get peaches.
Karma works this way.

Engaged renunciation
is treasuring simplicity within
a life of consciously loving,
working, and creating.

Come to realize that when you
are happy, you are in touch with
your greatest human potential.

Freedom is your greatest joy.

By learning how to be,
how to wake up, how to live
in the now, you learn how to
savor every drop of life. You may
find you don't want to waste
time distractedly stuffing food
down your throat or staring
at a really bad TV show or doing
all the other things you can
distract yourself with.

In every part and corner
of our life, to lose oneself
is to be a gainer, to forget
oneself is to be happy.
ROBERT LOUIS STEVENSON

Cultivate thoughts
that hasten the development
of wholesome qualities.

We reap what we sow.

Eat with moderation.

People who learn to control inner experience will be able to determine the quality of their lives, which is as close as any of us can come to being happy.
MIHALY CSIKSZENTMIHALYI

Remember, happiness can only be found within.

Happiness does not come from having much, but from being attached to little.

It is essential to learn
to enjoy life.

If you are not absolutely certain,
let go of assuming you know
something that you don't.
Embrace the not-knowing.

The secret of happiness
is that it is always a choice.

Remember that each of us is
endowed with Five Great
Blessings: happiness, health,
virtue, peace, and longevity.

Slow down and enjoy life.
It's not only the scenery
you miss by going too fast—
you also miss the sense of where
you're going and why.

We can have the happiness that
comes from not being attached,
from letting go of our craving
and allowing it to end.

Bring music into your
everyday activities.

Cultivate happiness!
I said briefly to the doctor:
Do you cultivate happiness?
How do you manage?
…Happiness is not a potato,
to be planted in mold and tilled
with manure.

A meaningful ethical system
divorced of an individual
experience of suffering and
happiness is hard to imagine.
DALAI LAMA

Aspire to live up to your happier
higher power.

See all appearances
as dazzling works as art.

Joy is a fruit of awakening
but also a prerequisite.

You allow life to surprise you. You allow life to be your teacher.

The little things in life are as interesting as the big ones.

What a relief it is for the burdened man who has long walked through the world of suffering to lay down his heavy and useless load.

Realize the joy and simplicity in being unencumbered by unnecessary possessions and incessant desires.

It's more productive and much more fun to respond creatively than to react cantankerously.

Do what you can with what you have, where you are.

If you stay with the moment, there is just enough time to do what needs to be done, just enough materials to complete the job as far as it needs completing.

Acting in skillful ways leads to happy results.

The happier you are, and the more free from stress, the better your food will taste.

The decision to be happy is actually the decision to stop being unhappy.

A reporter was asking the Dalai Lama on his recent visit to Washington, *You have written this book,* The Art of Happiness, *which was on the best-seller list for two years—could you please tell me and my readers about the happiest moment of your life?* And the Dalai Lama smiled and said, *I think now!*
DALAI LAMA

The secret of happiness is renunciation.
ANDREW CARNEGIE

To be without desire is to be content. But contentment is not happiness. And in contentment there is no progress. Happiness is to desire something, to work for it, and to obtain at least a part of it. In the pursuit of beloved labor the busy days pass cheerfully employed, and the still nights in peaceful sleep. For labor born of desire is not drudgery, but human play. Success brings hope, hope inspires fresh desire, and desire gives zest to life and joy to labor. This is true whether your days be spent in palaces of the powerful or in some little green by-way of the world. Therefore, while yet you have the strength, cherish a desire to do some useful work in your little corner of the world, and have the steadfastness to labor. For this is the way to the happy life; with health and endearing ties, it is the way to the glorious life.

From moment to moment
we are creating our future.
We are not a ball of dust tossed
about by the winds of fate.
We have full responsibility
for our lives.

The secret of contentment
is knowing how to enjoy
what you have, and to be able
to lose all desire for things
beyond your reach.

Make a habit of asking yourself,
*Is this task or behavior really
necessary or is it just a way to be
busy?* If you can reduce or
eliminate some activities, you
will achieve greater peace and
quiet, which is essential to
advancing in training.

First, let go of the idea that
things and experiences
can make you happy.

No matter what you are doing, keep the undercurrent of happiness. Learn to be secretly happy within your heart in spite of all circumstances.

Diligence, patience, and generosity bring us the conditions for happiness. Not having any sense of what hurts ourselves and others does not bring happiness.

Generating joyful effort every morning is a great way to start the day.

Prayer: *May the negative karma and suffering of all living beings ripen on me, and thus may they all be freed from suffering and its causes.*
GESHE KELSANG GYATSO

135

True happiness is to enjoy the present, without anxious dependence on the future.

Find and pursue your passion.

Tomorrow doesn't matter, for I have lived today.
HORACE

The poetic freshness of the present moment is the starting point.

True happiness is a condition of broad wisdom, boundless energy, and good fortune wherein you shape your own destiny, find fulfillment in daily activities, and come to understand your ultimate purpose in life.

Try to live your day in such a way that whenever you stop and look at the footprints you have made, you see a happy path and one that you will benefit from continuing to follow.

The true value of a human being can be found in the degree to which he has attained liberation from the self.
ALBERT EINSTEIN

If you can just stand still and let go, you have pure awareness.

137

Be so busy that you don't have time to look for happiness. Have work to do and be content with the work.

Each person in the chain of karma has a choice about how to act. They can choose whether or not to act on a seed of anger. Instead, they can counteract it with actions of strength, compassion, love, and self-confidence.

The great foolishness that people perpetuate is to make themselves unhappy because of their own reactions.

Every event and every situation in which you find yourself has a positive value.

Express your unique creativity.

By cultivating positive thoughts, you create the cause for a happy, peaceful state of mind.

Undertake for one week not to gossip positively or negatively—nor to speak about anyone you know who is not present.

Pleasure in moderation relaxes and tempers the spirit.
SENECA

There is a way to erase some of our negative karma: purification. This requires understanding that you have behaved badly in the past and that you must take full responsibility for this behavior. Then you must sincerely regret and repent your negative actions and promise yourself to try not to behave badly again. Finally, try to perform only positive, virtuous actions from now on.

Good actions bring happiness and bad actions bring misery.

Happiness is an endowment, not an acquisition. It depends more on temperament and disposition than on environment.

You can't stop the waves, but you can learn to surf.
JOSEPH GOLDSTEIN

If you can stay truly accepting as your world shifts and morphs, and if you can face it head on and stay alert and awake, the acceptance of change can take you to a high spiritual realization on its own.

The better you understand this flawed universe, the more skillfully you can live and the happier you will be.

According to the Buddha's teachings, the most basic condition for happiness is freedom—freedom from anger, despair, jealousy, delusion.

Practice consciously doing one thing at a time. Do whatever you're doing more slowly, more intentionally, and with more awareness and respect.

Value silence and its eloquence.

Make the most of all that comes and the least of all that goes.

Inhale negative karma, difficulties, conflicting emotions—exhale it as happiness and joy.

We should not be sure of any perception we have.
Ask: *Are you sure?*

Nonattachment to all sensations is the route to happiness.

When you are grounded in calmness and moment-to-moment awareness, you are more likely to be creative, see new options, find new solutions to problems, be aware of emotions and get less carried away by them, and be able to maintain your balance and perspective in trying circumstances.

Happiness is reflective,
like the light of heaven.
WASHINGTON IRVING

Your goal is to live in a simple,
direct way—without cluttering
up the mind with wanting things,
hating things, judging, taking
too much, worrying, or
doubting. It is the experience of
genuine happiness. Take it!

Celebrate life with fun
and laughter.

Happiness comes from acting
with the knowledge that you
don't have much time,
so you live with fullness,
attention, impeccability.

More important than anything else in the world is the intention to become liberated. When you have this, everything else falls into place perfectly.

Today well lived makes every yesterday a dream of happiness and every tomorrow a vision of hope.
SUFI PROVERB

Actions that lead not to distress, but to a heart bright and cheerful, are good karma. Knowing what karma is useful, one should act quickly thereon.
BUDDHA

Meet each experience with strength, softness, fluidity.

Forge a balanced and skillful approach to life, taking care to avoid extremes.

Don't think you are carrying the whole world on your shoulders. Even if you are, make it fun, make it easy, make it play.

You can't take wealth, possessions, or family with you—only your accumulated virtue, wisdom, and karma.

Begin your practice of generosity with giving away material things.

Get used to wiping the slate clean and never harboring grudges.

Your actions should demonstrate generosity, patience, awareness, wisdom, and discipline.

Create positive karma now!

The positive seed within you is your yearning to practice and wake up.

With wisdom and awareness, we can see that there are skillful activities that are conducive to greater happiness and understanding—and there are unskillful ones that lead to further suffering and conflict. Restraint is the capacity we have to discriminate one from the other, and the strength and composure of mind to pursue the skillful course.

Buddhist teacher Gehlek Rimpoche says: What is happiness?… Do you look for it somewhere in the sky or clouds?… When you look for happiness, look for pain, and when you find the pain, and you begin to see it lessening, you'll find happiness.

Concentrate on the now, and the future will take care of itself.

Nurture the roots of happiness.

Invite yourself to be happy in this moment.

Learn to get along with yourself so that you stop searching for happiness in someone else.

Look on each morning as a rebirth, and understand that only this one day exists. (But it doesn't mean rushing and doing as many things as you can.)

Ordinarily, we just cannot handle the natural joy of our mind, so we end up churning these intense emotions. The human mind by nature is joyous, calm, and very clear. From a Buddhist point of view, we are inherently peaceful.

The past and future do not exist, so how can they possibly make you happy?

If we are fully present in the moment, time will be suspended. That feeling of being trapped or overwhelmed will evaporate.

Many people think that if they were only in some other place, or had some other job, they would be happy. Well, that is doubtful. So get as much happiness out of what you are doing as you can and don't put off being happy until some future date.
DALE CARNEGIE

Write down ten things you are grateful for or happy about every morning.

Many eyes go through the meadow, but few see the flowers in it.
RALPH WALDO EMERSON

Favor products that are durable, easy to repair, nonpolluting in manufacture and use, energy-efficient, functional, and aesthetic.

151

Remind yourself that it is your thinking that is negative, not your life—an awareness that is a step toward happiness.

Our attachment to opinions and beliefs can never bring happiness.

Cultivating joy is another direct antidote to ill will. For example, when there is pain in your knee, contemplate the blessing of having a knee that functions.

A man's happiness and success in life will depend not so much on what he has, or on what position he occupies, as on what he is, and the heart he carries into his position.

152

Identify and water the positive seeds every day.

It is not the rich man you should properly call happy, but him who knows how to use with wisdom the blessings of the gods, to endure hard poverty, and who fears dishonor worse than death, and is not afraid to die for cherished friends or fatherland.
HORACE

We have a natural right to achieve as much happiness as possible, and we also have a right to overcome suffering.

Do things that create and reinforce happiness.

Open your eyes to the greatness of your world.

A well-spent day brings happy sleep.
LEONARDO DA VINCI

If you can look at situations with a balanced point of view, without attachment or indulging in harmful acts, you are living a proper life.

We can go through our whole lives worrying about our future happiness, and totally miss where true peace lives—right here, right now.

Realize that we all have the same potential of good and bad and that, therefore, it is important to use the good potential to be a happier human being.

Be in a happy swirl of doing.

When you are naturally elated, you don't feel like polluting your body. You feel like loving the body—and loving everything. When you feel good, food settles into its natural place in you.

Any positive change you make has the capacity to bear fruit.

If joy is to endure and mature serenely, it must be linked to other aspects of true happiness: clarity of mind, loving-kindness, the gradual withering of negative emotions, and the disappearance of selfish whimsy.

The law of karma shows you that the way to achieve happiness is by engaging in positive actions and refraining from negative ones. Not only do you yourself create the cause for your future happiness, but, by being kind, ethical, and compassionate toward others, you make yourself feel good about yourself while making those around you happy, too.

Life is ours to spend, not to be saved.
D.H. LAWRENCE

This moment is all we really have to work with. But we forget we are here. We are in the here-and-now.

Supreme happiness consists in self-content; that we may gain this self-content, we are placed upon this earth and endowed with freedom.
JEAN-JACQUES ROUSSEAU

Your actions are the result of past karma and the creation of new karma. Action creates memory and memory creates desire. Desire produces further action, which continues the cycle of karma. To be aware of this reality and to master your actions are the keys to creating the karma of happiness.

Choose being happy over being right.

To watch the corn grow, and the blossoms set; to draw hard breath over plowshare or spade; to read, to think, to love, to hope, to pray—these are the things that make us happy.

157

Being ignorant of the truth of dissatisfaction,
we believe that a new job, new house, or new partner
will bring us genuine happiness. Ignorant of how the energy
of our words and deeds travels with us from this life to the next,
we allow greed, hatred, doubt, and jealousy to motivate us.
Ignorant that a simple and disciplined life, good friends, meditation,
and mindful investigation of the true nature of our experience
will bring us happiness in this life and in lives to come, we make
millions of excuses for not engaging in these positive activities.

Strong people believe in cause and effect,
not luck or circumstance.

Loving

Love is the wish for all beings to experience happiness. It is not just romantic love or love for our family and friends. By cultivating an all-embracing love in your heart, you can spread happiness to many other people. When people are happy, their hearts open and they respond more lovingly to others. So approaching others with love in your heart means that they will be likely to respond in a loving manner to you. This helps create happiness all the way around. The love that wishes happiness for others also creates the karma cause for the happiness that you will experience in the future.

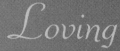

When a loved one dies,
they are gone. So let them go.
Didn't you love them fully while
they were here? Didn't you share
joy and laughter with them?
When something ends, let it.
It is the nature of this world.

To love someone
is to be happy with who
and what they are, accepting
them without conditions.

From a quiet, loving place, bless
all creation. Just quiet the mind
and send love out to the ends of
the universe, unconditionally.
What you give is what you get.
This is an exercise to strengthen
your ability to love.

Right underneath your thoughts
and negative emotions exists an
ocean of love. You have but to
quiet the mind to experience it.

Begin right now by engaging love and compassion however you can—not tomorrow, but today.

Teach happiness, teach love.

Show others how to love and be happy like you.

Practice loving-kindness to your tendency to eat mindlessly, to judge yourself, to feel impatient, angry, fearful.

Rahula, practice loving-kindness to overcome anger.
Loving-kindness has the capacity to bring happiness to others
without demanding anything in return. Practice compassion
to overcome cruelty. Compassion has the capacity to remove
the suffering of others without expecting anything in return.
Practice sympathetic joy to overcome hatred. Sympathetic joy arises
when one rejoices over the happiness of others and wishes others
well-being and success. Practice nonattachment to overcome
prejudice. Nonattachment is the way of looking at all things openly
and equally. This is because that is. Myself and others are not separate.
Do not reject one thing only to chase after another.
I call these the four immeasurables. Practice them,
and you will become a refreshing source
of vitality and happiness for others.
BUDDHA

Let the people in your life, especially your life partner, be as they are. They have to go through whatever their life demands of them. Love them without wanting them to be anything other than what they are. Love them without controlling them.

Patience is the mark of true love.

When our acts are motivated by generosity, love, or wisdom, then we are creating karmic conditions for abundance and happiness.

The love you experience at any time with any person is not coming from them: It's coming from inside of you. It is your experience of your true self. The other person is a stimulus that allows your own love to be uncovered.

Ask for help from those you trust
and from those whom you know
to be wise and compassionate.

What a person takes in
by contemplation,
she pours out in love.

Relationships do not provide
love. Love comes from within
you; it is your true, real nature.

Beyond being lovers,
you and your partner must be on
the same team, friends, focused
on a common yearning for
spiritual freedom.

If you want to be happy, the best thing you can do is thank, forgive, and consciously love your partner—and everyone else—for being themselves.

Any relationship has a better chance of surviving if you are not in it to get your desires filled, but to simply be loving. True love wants nothing except to love. It is the grace of true love when you can accept your whole self, your inadequacies, and your unconsciousness, as well as those of your partner.

Loving-friendliness, a sense of interconnectedness with all beings and a sincere wish for them to be happy, has far-reaching effects.

Loving requires no effort. Desperately wanting love is exhausting. Be the love you want, be the approval you want. Try loving the world and see how much easier your life gets.

Happiness cannot be traveled to, owned, earned, worn, or consumed. Happiness is the spiritual experience of living every minute with love, grace, and gratitude.

Be love. If you can, let go of wanting approval. Let go of wanting love. Give yourself some approval. Give yourself some love. This is enough. If you can let go of resisting who you are and allow yourself to be exactly as you are, you might feel a tremendous relief. That is loving yourself.

Radiating the warmth of love is pure simplicity; generating the cool rays of compassion is a relief.

Love is wanting others to be happy. It is a natural quality of mind, but until we develop it through meditation and other practices it remains limited, reserved for a few select individuals. Genuine love is universal in scope, extending to everyone, without exception.

KATHLEEN MCDONALD

We should enjoy the good things that come our way—for as long as they last.

Love completely, unselfishly, and unconditionally.

Loving-friendliness may improve a difficult job situation.

Speak truthfully with words that inspire self-confidence, joy, and hope.

On the other shore there are wholesome states that originate
from loving-kindness, compassion, joy, and equanimity.
So loving-kindness, compassion, joy, and equanimity are the first
wholesome states to be arisen. From them arise other wholesome
states as giving, generosity, helping to advance, consoling, sharing
the Dharma. These good things bring happiness. If we seek happiness,
we have to make them arise. We should remember that if we do not
live in goodness, we are not happy. To live with a sincere heart
is to live in peace. This is not a wish, but a fact.

True success is about satisfying your spirit with spirit things.
Your spirit doesn't want money for toys for your ego.
It wants joy, happiness, love.

Practice loving wishes
and cause reactive patterns
to lose strength, so you can
live with greater ease and
happiness and joy.

If you really love someone,
train yourself to be a listener.

Breathe out and send loving-
kindness to everyone,
including yourself.

Love is the ultimate way to
transform people, even when
they are full of anger and hatred.
You need tremendous patience to
do this continually and steadily.

Through your love for each other, through learning the art
of making one person happy, you learn to express your love for the
whole of humanity and all beings. Please help us develop the
curriculum for the Institute for the Happiness of One Person. Don't
wait until we open the school. You can begin practicing right away.

THICH NHAT HANH

A person who has nothing but loving feelings
will feel safe and secure, totally at ease,
because nothing can sway him.

No one who truly loves herself could harm another, for she would be harming herself.

Let us be grateful to people who make us happy: They are the charming gardeners who make our souls blossom.
MARCEL PROUST

To say we love someone is not enough, we also need to be tolerant and respectful.

Love is an outward movement from the heart that impels you to break out of narrow self-centeredness and open up to the whole world. Loving-kindness reminds you that acceptance is at the root of love. It is about gratitude for life, for your own existence, and for other people, without whom you would be alone.
MARTINE BATCHELOR

To love means to nourish another person with appropriate attention.

Love, laugh, delight, and hold onto nothing.

Love charitable acts for the happiness they bring to others.

Stop wanting.
The only way to become loving and to attain a loving state is to quiet the mind a bit.

More often than not, as you strengthen your ability to love consciously, the people in your life will change for the better without any effort on your part. It is as if you start resonating at a different frequency, and suddenly the people in your life start tuning into your channel.

Show children that one does not create happiness through indulgence.

Whatever one does must emerge from an attitude of love and benefiting others.
MILAREPA

Think of the impact—
of a happy, loving parent
on a child; of a happy, loving
teacher on a student.

The solution is not to deny attachment but to become less controlling in how we love.

The love that comes from wisdom is unconditional, universal loving-kindness— friendliness and warmth for all beings. Not looking to others for completion, not relating out of need.

What is most needed is a loving heart.
BUDDHA

Take the emphasis off getting love and put it on giving love.

Generating love and compassion is how we live our lives in full bloom.

Dwell on what is most lovable about a person. Value the merits of others.

It does not matter whether somebody did something for us or not, we can offer our love and compassion. Even by meeting someone else's eyes, we let go of where we're holding back.

Mothers and fathers who are calm and happy bring affection and a sense of caring into the lives of their children, thereby transforming society into something more compassionate and peaceful.

The more love we can extend, the more people we can include in it, the more love we have.

Our children love respect—they want respect for their needs and fears. With respect, we can offer our children protection and wholehearted nurturance, while achieving appropriate limits of others' hearts.

Abandon thoughts of blame and hate, and live in love.

If you give the gifts of love, compassion, and wisdom from your heart, your generosity will bear the fruit of happiness.

Love many things.

Believe in yourself! Have faith in your abilities! Without a humble but reasonable confidence in your own powers you cannot be successful or happy.
NORMAN VINCENT PEALE

The smallest gift given purely with love creates more happiness than an expensive gift given resentfully, or with the expectation of receiving something in return.

Joy comes not from possession or ownership, but through a wise and loving heart.

Becoming a more loving person in our everyday relationships may be one of the most compassionate actions we can do—becoming a little kinder.

When you feel love and kindness toward others, it not only makes others feel loved and cared for, but it also helps you to develop inner happiness and peace.

If you find a good companion who is following the same spiritual path, then travel together, overcoming obstacles as they arise.

Love those whom no one else loves.

When you are with the person you love, be with the person you love without expecting anything.

To live in love is to live in joy.

Generosity is the willingness to give, to share, to let go. Love is the inspiration; and, in giving, you feel more love.

Love, and love alone, is capable of giving thee a happier life.

BEETHOVEN

Our home, children, and body are given to us for a short while—to treat with care and respect.

As you begin consciously loving, you may find that you have more energy, feel happier, and find that people will generally be very nice to you. Conscious loving does not work if you have an agenda.

When you realize that at some point there will be an ending, you might see how precious each moment is and embrace your love with that much more passion. Take nothing for granted. Enjoy it while you can, because it will end.

From the Buddhist perspective, love is the wish for all beings to experience happiness.

Happiness, then, is the confidence that pain and disappointment can be tolerated, that love will prove stronger than aggression. It is release from the attachment to pleasant feelings, and faith in the capacity of awareness to guide us through the inevitable insults to our own narcissism. It is the realization that we do not have to be so self-obsessed, that within our own minds lies the capacity for a kind of acceptance we had only dreamed of. This happiness rarely comes without effort to train the mind.

MARK EPSTEIN

Happiness and love
come naturally in letting go
of fear.

You have to generate love for yourself first.

The person who practices loving speech and deep listening is practicing peace.

If you are present for your partner without expectation, grasping, attachment, or need, then you are doing everything you can do. If you love somebody, set them free. Love—and let the rest go.

The person we love needs space in order to be happy.

I will cherish all living beings without exception because this precious mind of love is the supreme method for solving all problems and fulfilling all wishes. Eventually it will give me the supreme happiness of enlightenment.
GESHE KELSANG GYATSO

Let kindness, generosity, love, and wisdom motivate your intentions—and happiness will follow.

Only here and now can we truly love—the past is a memory, the future is a fantasy.

The sanctuary of a loving relationship provides encouragement and sustenance to stay focused on the truth: It's precious to have that kind of partner, especially in a world of distractions.

Appreciate your happy relationships and accept your imperfect relationships.

Clinging is not the same as loving. It is not the same as caring for someone's welfare and wanting that person to be happy. It is, rather, a jealous or obsessive possessiveness that seeks to own another person. Some try to possess each other, are bossy or controlling—and strangle the relationship. Clinging to anything makes us unhappy.

When you realize you are loved, love will fly to you from every direction. As long as you are in a lacking mind-set, you are a lack magnet.

Life is a paradise for those who love many things with a passion.
LEO BUSCAGLIA

Share the best of yourself through your words—your joy, your love. Try to avoid sharing the worst of yourself—your blaming, criticizing, judgmental words. Use your words to support, not tear down.

If you truly love someone, you will want that person to be happy, whether or not their happiness depends on you.

You must take care of yourself; loving-kindness is the answer.

Support happiness and you will teach love, peace, acceptance.

To love what you do and feel that it matters—how could anything be more fun?
KATHERINE GRAHAM

In this life, we cannot do great things. We can only do small things with great love.

Once you contact your capacity for love and happiness, the light has been turned on.

Aware of the suffering caused by unmindful speech and the inability to listen to others, I am committed to cultivating loving speech and deep listening in order to bring joy and happiness to others and relieve others of their suffering. Knowing that words can create happiness or suffering, I am determined to speak truthfully, with words that inspire self-confidence, joy, and hope. I will not spread news that I do not know to be certain, and will not criticize or condemn things of which I am not sure. I will refrain from uttering words that can cause the family or the community to break. I am determined to make all efforts to reconcile and resolve all conflicts, however small.

If we cultivate loving-kindness, we experience it
in the moment and strengthen it as a force in the mind,
making it easier for it to arise again.

The blessings that come from cultivating loving-kindness are:
Your dreams become sweet. You fall asleep easily. You waken
contented. Your thoughts are pleasant. Your health improves.
Angels and other divine beings will love and protect you. Animals
will sense your love and not harm you. People will welcome you
everywhere. Your babies will be happy. If you lose things, they will be
returned. If you fall off a cliff, a tree will be there to catch you.
The world will be more peaceful around you.

The truth is that every soul is already mated in the highest, most divine way. Truly finding your soul mate is finding yourself.

When you start to pay attention, your relationship to things changes. You see more and you see more deeply. Knowing what you are doing while you are doing it is the essence of mindfulness practice.

Love is accepting. Love is allowing of how another chooses to be. Love is a feeling of bliss and pure joy and acceptance of another being, of the world, and of yourself. The reward of being in a loving state is the greatest reward possible: just being in a loving state.

Be in the present moment with the one you love, without assuming or expecting anything. Being present for your partner is the greatest gift you can give.

I will greet this day with love in my heart. And how will I do this?
Henceforth will I look on all things with love and I will be born again.
I will love the sun for it warms my bones; yet I will love the rain for it
cleanses my spirit. I will love the light for it shows me the way;
yet I will love the darkness for it shows me the stars. I will welcome
happiness for it enlarges my heart; yet I will endure sadness
for it opens my soul. I will acknowledge rewards for they are my due;
yet I will welcome obstacles for they are my challenge.

You will notice that the happier you are,
the more loving you are.

The whole thrust is to become more loving and compassionate without expecting or hoping for anything in return.

Restraining yourself and loving others are seeds that bear fruit in this life and beyond.
NAGARJUNA

Cultivating a loving response to others at all times, whatever their attitude toward us, creates the karma that results in our receiving love and happiness in the future.

Communicate unconditional love.

191

Unlock the habit of clinging—
which occurs when we are
unhappy or feeling inadequate.

Fully appreciate the learning and
love that life offers us in each
moment, to feel less desire for
material luxuries that deprive
others of scarce resources.

Love and hard work changes you
into someone who lives in joy.

If you love everything,
you will perceive the divine
mystery in things.
DOSTOYEVSKY

Success is a twinkle in the eye, a generosity of spirit, a palpable energy projected from a loving heart, and a caring soul.

Practice being more loving, more aware, more conscious.

Always love and support your partner. Your partner is you and you are your partner, so be helpful, be loving.

Learn to be secretly happy within your heart, in spite of all circumstances.

Meditating for Happiness

The evidence of the positive effect of meditation on well-being is quite impressive. Regular meditation can reduce negative emotions, and mindfulness linked with meditation has been shown to reduce stress, improve immune responses, and increase overall well-being. The increase in awareness from meditation can make an incredible difference in your life, in terms of your own happiness as well as the happiness of those around you. Meditation teaches you to be mindful and honest, which makes your mind quieter and more open, your heart happier and more peaceful.

Breathing in, make your mind happy and at peace. Breathing out, make your mind happy and at peace.

The path of meditation is dedicated to the discovery of peace in each moment.

Take a few minutes, either at home or on your way to work, to notice something enjoyable about the morning.

Pick happy thoughts to meditate on.

Take some moments in your day when your mind is calm and consciously invite into those spaces one of these simple questions: What is happiness? What more do I need in this moment to be free? What is peace? What do I need to let go of or be at peace with a certain person, event, or memory? What am I clinging to? Listen to the responses that rise up, but let go of the need for answers or resolution. Stay with the question. If the mind becomes agitated, let go of the question and stay on the breath or other sounds. When you are calm, return to the question.

It is the yogic way to go through a problem, not away from it. Aim for the center, take a deep breath, and dive in. Nothing is what it seems once you are inside. The deeper you dive, the closer you get to the truth that everything is consciousness, and that everything and everyone is precious and lovable. You develop a kind of heightened vision that allows you to see through the surface to underneath, where there is love.

One minute of meditation practice is one minute of generating the energy of mindfulness.

Toward the ultimate yogic goal of enlightenment, this undoing of worry creates space for bliss and joy to gain momentum in your life, until eventually uninterrupted happiness becomes your predominant state.

Taming your mind is not a hobby or an extracurricular activity—it is the most important thing you could be doing. It can even help streamline a pressured situation because it gives you clarity, peace, and fortitude. You may need to simplify your life in order to meditate, but a benefit of meditation is that it will make your life simpler.

If the physical practice of yoga is accompanied by a deeper spiritual practice, the flow of energy gains momentum, creating a cycle that keeps swelling until you have more energy than a hummingbird and you're lit up like a lightbulb.

You have to do *zazen* every day, or desires can get a stronger foothold.
Remind yourself through *zazen* how fulfilled you already are,
and you'll have an easier perspective about all the things
you think you want. You'll see how much you really don't need it.
You'll learn to feel good about what you have and enjoy finding ways
to get by on less. And you'll feel more content.

In the car, do a loving-kindness meditation. Say to other drivers:
*May you safely reach your destination. May you find the happiness and
fulfillment that you are seeking.* As with any meditation practice,
when you notice that your attention has wandered, gently smile to
yourself, take a deep breath, and refocus your mind back into the
meditation that you are doing.

As you go to bed and prepare for sleep, take some mindful breaths, become aware of the bed supporting you, and allow yourself to smile. Feel the muscles of your body relaxing as you sink into your bed.

Focus your attention inward.

Even a few minutes in quiet meditation can calm your mind and open your heart, bringing you more deeply into the moment.

Yoga is about revealing happiness. Yoga means union, union with your own inherent radiant happiness. You can only BE that happiness. So be it!

Through truth seeking and yoga practice,
you allow life force to flow through in abundance.
When this happens, unconditional love gushes forth.
Bad feelings will be replaced by unconditional love and forgiveness.

Sit down, relax. Breathe and smile. Be happy and peaceful.
Practice the laughing Buddha, smiling yoga meditation. Smile.
Smile even more. Smile as if you were enlightened. Grin. Be silly.
Relax your mind. Be happy. See how that feels. Imagine what it
looks like. Awakened Buddha, smile happily.

Meditation is a way to let the silt settle back to the bottom,
so we can see the fish.

Meditation for happiness and extending one's life:
Sit comfortably with your palms facing. Curl the fingers of your left
hand into a fist and wrap the fingers of your right hand around the left,
heels of the hands touching. Bring your thumbs together,
resting them on the index finger of the left hand and not touching
the right index finger. With the hands eight to ten inches
from the face at mouth level, begin inhaling deeply through
the nose and exhaling through the mouth, directing air through the
opening created naturally by the hand position. Do this for eleven
minutes or as long as you wish, even until you fall asleep.

We have to learn the art of breathing in and out, stopping our activities, and calming our emotions. We have to learn to become solid and stable like an oak tree, not blown side to side by a storm.

Take your time eating and be very happy.

One who drinks deep the Dharma lives happily with a tranquil mind.
BUDDHA

Purposefully stop all the doing in your life and relax into the present without trying to fill it up with anything.

If you breathe in and out and feel joy and peace,
that's Right Diligence.

Meditation for remembering the good in you: Sit and close your eyes.
Let go of analysis and expectation. Bring to mind something you have
done or said that you feel was a kind or good action. When it comes to
mind, be with the happiness that may come with the memory. If a kind
or good action does not come to mind, then focus on a quality you like
about yourself. Otherwise, reflect on your urge to have happiness. Be
with what is happening, but do not get involved with desire or
aversion. Let go and begin again, just being with the meditation.

Just being, returning to original nature, is expanded consciousness. To do that, we have to become very quiet, very still—to enter into a state of merging.

With meditation central to your being, your life is free from suffering.

Happy or sad, energetic or tired, just sit as the being you happen to be right now.

Find joy in the sweetness of surrender, the stillness of meditation.

Serenity prayer: *God grant me the serenity to accept the things I cannot change; courage to change the things I can; and wisdom to know the difference. Living one day at a time; Enjoying one moment at a time; Accepting hardships as the pathway to peace; Taking, as He did, this sinful world as it is, not as I would have it; Trusting that He will make all things right if I surrender to His Will; That I may be reasonably happy in this life and supremely happy with Him Forever in the next. Amen.*

The more meditation you do,
the more you get in touch with yourself naturally.
You become more aware of what you are doing
on a moment-by-moment basis.

By learning to hold our mind to an object in meditation,
we train in patience. Then when a moment of anger arises
in our everyday life, we might be able to hold our speech and action.
We don't jump, lash, or act out. If we are really dedicated
to practicing patience, we even learn to generate love
and compassion on the spot when anger arises.

We have to learn the art of stopping—
stopping our thinking, our habit energies, our forgetfulness,
the strong emotions that rule us.

Meditation for having compassion for the person you hate or despise the most: Sit, breathe, and smile a half-smile. Contemplate the person you hate or despise most. Bring to mind what features you hate or despise most about him or her. Try to examine what makes this person happy and what causes suffering in his or her daily life. Try to see what patterns of thought and reason this person follows, what motivates this person's actions. Consider whether this person's consciousness, views, and insights are open and free or are influenced by prejudices, narrow-mindedness, hatred, or anger. Is this person the master of himself or herself? Continue until you feel some compassion rise in your heart. Practice this exercise many times on the same person.

Let the Buddha speak through you with healing words of acceptance, love, compassion.

Practice means being in the present on purpose.

Try giving a label to inspiring thoughts that occur during meditation, as they arise like Einstein!

Meditating while working makes clear the most fundamental of Zen principles: that meditation is not merely a matter of learning to focus and concentrate your mind during meditation, but rather a matter of bringing that state into even the smallest acts of our daily life.

You must learn to be still in the midst of activity and to be vibrantly alive in repose.
INDIRA GANDHI

The yoga triangle, or happy pose, allows joy to fill your body and radiate from within you.

When you are happy, meditate for a few moments and be grateful for that feeling.

Try meditating on an image that you associate with happiness or peace for a few minutes before you go to bed. This may ward off bad dreams.

Our heart and mind are inherently awake for dealing with the rigors of life, and the mind of meditation is a wonderful ally.

What does it take to be happy? True happiness arises when we are able to change our minds rather than the world around us, when we loosen the bonds of self-focus enough to care more for others.

Willingly practice mental and physical disciplines that lead to greater freedom, skill, and joy.

Take a moment to assess whether it is beneficial to join in or rest in stillness.

Meditation can help us to uncover and develop the compassion that already exists within us. Meditation requires concentration and inquiry to deepen our awareness. From the clarity and understanding that comes from awareness, compassion for all beings arises spontaneously.

Meditation is to be aware of each feeling. Recognize it, smile to it, look deeply into it, and embrace it with all your heart.

Test the law of affirmation: If you can affirm something deeply, totally, and absolutely, it starts becoming real. That is why people are happy; they affirm joy. That is why people are miserable; they affirm misery. Make it a point to stop affirming the negative and start affirming the positive. It is a magic key.

Sit as usual. Set aside thoughts, concerns, and worries. Search in your current experience for the place inside where you feel happy or joyful. Merge with that feeling and let it permeate your whole being. Continue this as long as you can. Then open your eyes and carry this feeling with you throughout the day.

We can sense the ever-changing waves around us and breathe and relax. We can rest in the eternal present. We can learn that no matter what happens, we are home.

The next time you feel pulled in many different directions by your spouse or partner, children, and so forth, take a moment to draw a deep breath and experience a flash of silence before reacting (or instead of it).

Returning our mind to the breath is how we learn to be mindful and aware. Like giving a child a pet, caring for a living creature teaches us responsibility and loving-kindness.

If you practice mindful walking and deep listening all day long, that is the Four Noble Truths in action.

When you are surrounded by your normal chaos, it can become a battle, but that is the most important time to practice what you learn in meditation and yoga.

Repeated good intentions can generate a powerful inner voice that will keep you on track.

Meditation is the balance of awareness, concentration, and energy—a moment-to-moment balancing.

Take a few mindful breaths before you open a door.

Unify the mind through quiet and calm practice, so it is free, stable, unbound, centered.

Meditate on happiness. Just let whatever thoughts and images come to your mind be there. When they trail off, turn your senses within and meditate on what your real happiness is. You will know when you find it, because you will feel a deep, ecstatic inner glow. Slowly relax and return to normal. The inner glow of happiness will continue with you for some time. Take a moment and attune yourself to it.

Say: *May All Beings Be Awake,*
May All Beings Be Happy,
May All Beings Be at Peace.

Meditation is a way of paying attention and savoring one sense at a time.

Zazen transforms dryness, rigidity, and self-centeredness to warmth, resiliency, and compassion; self-indulgence and fear become self-mastery and courage.

It is true that practicing yoga tones and cleanses all the organs, detoxifies the body, increases circulation, oxygenates the body, balances the hormones, and prevents physical injuries—but that's only the beginning. Joy must be in the equation somewhere, otherwise it is not true yoga.

The practice of yoga postures alone is enough to significantly dilate the energetic pathways, which is why after a physical practice you are likely to feel so peaceful, powerful, and alive.

215

Stop! Every so often, just stop what you are doing and breathe—noticing the world all around you. Open your senses to the environment. Experience the present moment in complete stillness.

Practice also benefits from having a healthy body. Yoga and other forms of physical exercise contribute to our mental health.

Laugh while you practice! Smile at people! Bravely embrace your true experience. It is absolutely essential to be conscious. It is this self-awareness that will naturally take you to the next step, to deeper and longer periods of pure, simple, and perfect uninterrupted happiness.

A few relaxed breaths can make a big difference.

It only takes one conscious breath to be in touch with ourselves and the world around us.

The practice of yoga stimulates and accelerates the opening of rivers of energy and magnifies the life force, thereby enhancing its positive effects.

The body is meant to be a vehicle for joy, not suffering. Take care of your body and then forget about it. Don't obsess over body image, but don't let it stagnate either. Your body has the potential to bring you big fun if you let it.

Take a few moments each day to think carefully about the good things you have. Anything: good relationships, special skills, fine health, or happy children.

Dedication: *Due to the positive potential I have created with my meditative practice today, may anyone I meet abide in happiness forever. May each person find peace and happiness.*

We need to practice mindful breathing, deep listening, and deep looking.

Five minutes of practice with the sincere desire to wake up to the present moment is worth more than a lifetime of practice without it.

As you prepare to start your day, envision a large, happy lion stretching and roaring. Raise your arms and spread them wide with the palms forward. Stretch. Breathe. Like the lion, leap forward into your day.

Meditate on love and compassion
and stabilize the awakening mind.

Try a meditation on "I am happy/I am sad."
Relax and then use this contradictory statement or another like
"I am tired/I am alert." Visualize one half as clearly as possible.
If you choose "I am happy," picture yourself feeling this way
mentally and physically. Then do the other half. Go back and forth
between the two and try to feel how neither is completely true.
Then just say "I am" to yourself, sinking deeply into the sense
of I am and experiencing how true that seems.
Try to observe the sensation of I am.

Take a moment—stop in midactivity to find your center, regroup, remind yourself of what is important, who you are, where you are, what you are doing, what you can and can't control, and what is really happening now.

Equanimity meditation: Generate equanimity toward others by reciting phrases like...*All beings are the owners of their karma. Their happiness and unhappiness depend on their actions, not my wishes for them.* Or you can say: *May we all accept things as they are. May we remain undisturbed by changing events.* You first offer equanimity to a neutral person, then to your benefactor, a friend, an enemy, yourself, all beings, and so on.

One moment of practice becomes lasting pleasure.

Transform sorrow into compassion by meditating this way, saying: *May I be free from pain and sorrow. May I be happy and be at peace.*
Repeat for others you know.

In solitude we gain peace and balance, like the wind not caught by any net.

Simply relax and be happy.

Meditation siphons off the pools of old collected experience, allowing us to skillfully and compassionately act in the present rather than react to the past.

A pebble in your pocket can serve as a teacher, as a fellow practitioner—a "mindfulness bell"—allowing you to pause and return to your breathing.

End a meditation practice period by saying: *May I be peaceful, May I be happy, May all beings be peaceful, May all beings be happy.*

You want to remain in a state of perpetual meditation—total awareness, mindfulness, full immersion in the present moment: the ultimate in Zen living.

Calmly watching your breath come and go is the basic form of meditation that helps you become more in touch with the present.

With amusement and great affection, patiently gather your mind back again and again as gently and lovingly as you would a puppy.

Metta prayer: *May (I /other person) be filled with loving kindness. May (I/other person) be well. May (I/other person) be peaceful and at ease. May (I/other person) be happy.*

Metta prayer: *May I be balanced and at peace. May I be undisturbed by the comings and goings, of all the events of the world. May I be peaceful.*

Opening the body's energy pathways through physical yoga practice, inner yoga practice, directing your attention (and life force) into the body, and actually enjoying whichever practice you do—all will keep the body youthful, the mind peaceful, and you very, very happy.

The essence of *tonglen* is to breathe in the suffering of another person and to breathe out loving-kindness, compassion, and healing.

Make each activity of your day meditation.

You do not need to leave your room. Remain sitting at your table and listen. Do not even listen, simply wait. Do not even wait, be quite still and solitary. The world will freely offer itself to you unmasked, it has no choice, it will roll in ecstasy at your feet.
FRANZ KAFKA

Compose yourself in stillness;
draw your attention inward.

If you practice returning again
and again to the moment,
little by little you will taste
awareness. It tastes like joy.

Before you go to sleep,
make a list of ten things that
made you feel happy during the
day that just passed.
Not big things; the little things.

If you want to experience your
own inherent happiness,
do lots of yoga.

When we meditate, we learn that understanding is the essence of love and forgiveness. A person who is not happy will do or say things that make other people unhappy. Our happiness, based on compassion, will benefit others.

To a realized yogi, life looks absolutely perfect just as it is. Have faith and trust that the magic of cause and effect takes everyone through exactly what they need to go through, when they need to do so. If you see life as beautiful and miraculous, the world will show you that over and over again.

Daily affirmations to try: *I am becoming happier. The core of my being is at peace. Each experience I have is an opportunity for greater growth. There are no mistakes, only lessons. I forgive all who have hurt me. I forgive myself for all I have hurt. I go forth in love and peace. I embrace the universe. I send loving thoughts to all living beings.*

Wake up—again and again. It's a lifelong process. Let Zen be both a process and a pattern for your life.

Sit and become silent. In a simple way, review your current life. Review major areas like your schedule, work, finances, relationships, home, leisure activities, possessions, goals, and spiritual life.

Ask: *What would it be like to greatly simplify this area of my life?*

Sit and reflect, just letting images or answers arise.

After some time, then ask: *If it became simpler, would I be happy?*

Set a timer for five minutes and take a break from resisting your world.

Ask, *Can I allow myself to be exactly as I am, right in this moment?*

Allow everything about you to be exactly as it is—idiosyncrasies, regrets, physical shape, size, everything. Resist nothing. This is loving yourself. Then start setting the timer for twenty-four hours a day.

Look within; be still.

Relax, limber up, be sillier,
take fewer things seriously,
climb more mountains,
have fewer imaginary troubles,
travel lighter.

Commune with nature
and learn from it.

Happiness is there if you know
how to breathe and smile.

Do a brief meditation for cultivating compassion
when you are having difficulty with a loved one or friend.
Sit, looking beyond the conflict, and reflect on the fact that
this person is a human being like you. This person has the same desire
for happiness and well-being, the same fear of suffering, the same need
for love. Note how this meditation softens your feelings.

By taking yourself into the quiet and allowing
your awareness to go deeper than the everyday chaos,
you are developing a true yoga practice.

Do a *metta* practice: *May I be free from danger.*
May I have mental happiness. May I have physical happiness.
May I have ease of well-being. After offering these wishes to yourself,
go on to wishing them for others and then for the universe.

Gatha for rising: Waking up this morning, I smile.
Twenty-four brand new hours are before me.
I vow to live fully in each moment and
to look at all beings with eyes of compassion.

Know you are breathing in. Know you are breathing out.
Be aware of a pleasant feeling arising. Hold this feeling as though
it were your most precious child. Smile with joy at your happiness.
Then be aware of an unpleasant feeling arising. Be aware that you
dislike this feeling. Hold this feeling as though it too were your
most precious child. Smile with compassion at your suffering.
Be aware of the feeling's arising and then passing away.
Dwell in the present moment.

By watching the mind with vigilance, seeking the truth about yourself
tirelessly, and allowing and going through your fears as they arise,
you will find that your level of awareness subtly heightens.
When enlightenment is attained gradually, it is integrated
into daily life gently, naturally.

Your visions will become
clear only when you can look
into your own heart.
Who looks outside, dreams;
who looks inside, awakes.
CARL JUNG

Live one meditative day well,
with freedom, strength,
and wisdom.

Meditation works like one
of those snow domes—it helps
the flaky stuff of your mind settle
down, so you can see more
clearly what you truly need
and want.

Every moment of meditation is a
golden opportunity for a fuller,
happier life. Feel totally entitled
to your meditation period.

Capable of practicing silence, we are free as a bird, in touch
with the essence of things. Sometimes we have to practice silence.
Silence is a time for looking deeply. There are times when silence
is truth, and that is called "thundering silence."

You can feel happy coming back to the breath.
Don't worry that you are going to have to do it a thousand times.
That is why this is called *practice*.

233

Try to be happy in your practice,
to be satisfied with your life.

Try this visualization technique: Remain calm and reasonable.
Imagine another version of yourself who is egotistically self-centered.
Also imagine a group of poor people unrelated to you, who are needy
and suffering. Be calm and unbiased as you observe these two.
Be aware that both want happiness, both want to be rid of suffering,
and both have the right to accomplish these goals. Consider that we
often work long and hard, willing to make temporary sacrifices for a
long-term goal. By the same logic, one person could make sacrifices in
order to help a larger good. This would benefit a greater number of
people. The point is that you must serve and help other beings.

Using Mindfulness for Happiness

You are alive now. Reminding yourself of this helps you to cultivate mindfulness and to live your life both fully and well. When you are focused on the present moment, you are mindful and aware of your actions of body, mind, and speech. Being mindful and aware will help you to act skillfully so that you can create good karma, the seeds of future and lasting happiness. Being mindful of your experiences as they arise allows you to observe each sensation purely and immediately. Being with your experiences in the moment can reduce suffering and deepen the simple pleasure and happiness of being alive.

Bide your time and express
yourself effectively at the right
time, at the right place,
with the right words
and the right attitude!

In thinking, keep to the simple.

Quiet your thoughts.
By ruling them,
you find happiness.

Mindfulness helps us not to be
angry at our loved ones, because
we understand that they,
too, are suffering.

If with a pure mind
a person speaks or acts,
happiness follows him like his
never-departing shadow.
BUDDHA

Mindfulness is loving all
the details of our lives.

When the mind is not your
servant, when it is running
without your authorization, then
it is being dysfunctional. So
unless you need it for something,
turn it off. Learning how to shut
it off is the most important and
empowering thing you can do.
When you can get the mind
quiet, then there is a real chance
for a peaceful existence.

Chew your food very carefully
and with a lot of joy.

If our mind is pure and peaceful, we shall be happy regardless of our external circumstances.
GESHE KELSANG GYATSO

When we point and focus our minds toward the breath, the effort counteracts dullness and drowsiness. Anchoring the mind on an object drives away doubt. Rapture shuts out ill will. Happiness excludes restlessness and worry.

Rest in openness: Consciously do nothing, take it easy alertly, repose in wide-awakeness.

Your mind is the perfect Buddha.

Giving conscious attention to our actions and their consequences
makes them a potent source of learning.

Think for yourself, and, more importantly, feel for yourself.
What is beautiful to you? Why not decide for yourself how
your body can be the best experience for you? Why not let go
of trying to win everyone's approval or conform to a fashion?
Why not just listen to your own insight? If you feel good, anyone who
sees you will be drawn to you, no matter what your shape and size.

Try on occasion to eat in silence, slowly and mindfully.

Practice scanning your body with a beam of mindfulness.

Pay attention to what's happening right now. When you wash a glass, know it.

There is integrity in being certain that you do not know, and there is a space in your awareness for real wisdom to find its way in. Some call it thinking with the heart. Every moment is perfect, even in its imperfections.

Mindfulness can help you to overcome temptation, avoid quarrels, and respond compassionately to others' moral failings as well as your own.

Each moment of nonwanting is a moment of freedom. Mindfulness allows nonwanting. When there is clear attention, when there is just watching, there's not wanting.

Every moment can be used to gain insight, and from that calm arises.

Beginning again is an important part of this practice and is one of the great muscle builders of mindfulness.

We must first empty our minds
of premade thoughts.
Only when we dump out our
teacup can we make room for
the really good tea.

Practice mindful breathing
so that the time spent washing
the dishes is pleasant and
meaningful. Do not feel you have
to rush, or you waste the time
of dish washing.

Much more power is generated
by the ability to practice
awareness in the midst
of the world.

Try to be mindful of your
traveling. Take a few mindful
breaths to relax your body and
mind. Do your best to allow your
steps and actions to be peaceful
ones. Relax your shoulders,
soften your face.

If you spend your energy getting to know yourself, living mindfully, refusing to get caught up in petty details and behaviors, and living your life with integrity and compassion, people will probably respect you.

We can train our minds to find happiness with what is.

Calm the mind,
let go of the chatter,
and allow a stillness to fall.

Objects of consumption are always changing—as are our desires for the objects we consume. Look deeply into your way of consuming. When you take time to live mindfully, you will discover that living a simple life and consuming less are the true conditions for happiness.

Cultivate the energy of mindfulness with mindful breathing and walking. Use these simple, everyday acts to calm your emotions and nourish your joy.

Work within your own mind to attain happiness and to pacify suffering.

Listening is an art. When you listen with a still and concentrated mind, it is possible to be responsive to what is being said.

The instrument for watering wholesome seeds is mindful living—mindful breathing, mindful walking, living each moment of our day in mindfulness.

Mindfulness helps you respond appropriately in the moment. You can sometimes catch a stress reaction and turn it into a response instead.

Being aware and mindful of your actions will help you to act skillfully so that you create good karma, the seeds of future and lasting happiness.

We should welcome those moments when we can apply the brakes, take a deep breath, and gather ourselves before proceeding anew.

Learn to have relaxed control over your mind—through understanding the real causes of happiness and fulfillment.

It is beautiful and peaceful to stay in a place of silence of mind.

By waking up fully to each moment, we can learn to be awake and alive in ordinary life. Then ordinary life becomes something extraordinary.

To stop and pay attention to what is happening in the moment is one way of snapping out of…fixations. It is also a reasonable definition of meditation.
STEPHEN BATCHELOR

Once you live your life in awareness, you will live in true happiness.

Joy creates spaciousness in the mind that allows one to hold suffering without being overwhelmed or collapsing into helplessness or despair.

When our thoughts leave our mind in the form of speech, if Right Mindfulness continues to accompany them, we know what we are saying and whether it is useful or creating problems.

The more we are mindful of our thoughts, speech, and actions, the more concentration, insight into the nature of our own suffering, and the suffering of others arise. We then know what to do and what not to do in order to live joyfully and in peace with our surroundings.

If happiness comes, don't become too excited. If sorrow comes, don't become too depressed. Happiness and sorrow are not you. Watch, unattached. Happiness and suffering are dependent on your own mind, on your interpretation. They do not come from outside, from others.

The happiness of concentration makes possible
the next kind of happiness, the happiness of beginning insight.
When the mind is still, we can employ it in the service of awareness
and come to a deeper understanding of who we are and what life is
about. Wisdom unfolds in a very ordered way. When we sit and pay
attention to our experience, the first level we come to is psychological
insight. We see all our different sides—the loving side, the greedy side,
the judging side, the angry side, the peaceful side. We see parts of
ourselves that have been covered up—the jealousy, the fear, the
hatred, the unworthiness. Often when we first open up to the
experience of who we are, we don't like a lot of it. The tendency
is to be self-judgmental. Through the power of concentration and
mindfulness, we learn how to rest very naturally in the simple
awareness of what's happening. We become less judgmental.
We begin to get insight into the complexities of our personality.
We see the patterns of our thoughts and emotions, and the ways
we relate to people. But this is a tricky point in the practice.
Psychological insights can be very seductive—who's more
interesting than oneself?—so it's easy to get lost on this level
of inquiry. We need to be watchful and keep coming back
to the main object of meditation.

JOSEPH GOLDSTEIN

You can reflect on what you truly need in order to be happy. Be with anything that comes into your mind, and observe.

With awareness and calm comes a feeling of having more room to move, of having more options, of being free to choose effective and appropriate responses in stressful situations.

Remember to connect to what you are doing. Each moment that you remember, you are on the path to freedom.

Hold in your mind the idea of happiness, and imagine yourself being happy from the inside out. To be happy, you must see yourself as happy. Rehearse this state of happiness throughout the day. You can also do this for other things like love and peace.

The moment one gives close attention to anything, even a blade of grass, it becomes a mysterious, awesome, indescribably magnificent world in itself.
HENRY MILLER

Living Zen means to open yourself to a full awareness of your surroundings and yourself. You can use the storms, winds, and waves to propel you through life. You must lose yourself and become one with the boat, water, and wind.

We live immersed in a world of constant doing. To get back in touch with being is not that difficult. We remind ourselves to be mindful. Moments of mindfulness are moments of peace and stillness, even in the midst of activity.

Being precise in your awareness helps to tease apart the tangling of thoughts and feelings and to dispel the illusion of their solidness.

When you touch base in any moment with that part of your mind that is calm and stable, your perspective immediately changes. You can see things more clearly and act from inner balance.

Happiness is not a matter of events; it depends on the tides of the mind.

The practice of mindfulness meditation increases your capacity to stop and be present. You naturally develop deeper concentration and the capacity to look deeply into yourself or whatever you encounter.

You can nourish your mindfulness by doing anything you truly enjoy, like cooking or gardening.

Pay attention—give loving-kindness to your speech and your actions and the movements of your mind.

Wonderful, indeed, it is to subdue the mind, so difficult to subdue, ever swift, and wandering wherever it desires. A tamed mind brings happiness.
BUDDHA

Finding beauty in the ordinary, and the ordinary in beauty, is Zen living in action.

Train the mind in the direction of having enough, in being free, and you realize that the sense of hunger that you used to cultivate is a major source of suffering. You are much better off without it.

Don't let a distracted mind and thirsty senses search in vain for happiness in the pleasures of the world.

Examine your own actions and notice where you can make improvements in yourself rather than criticize the actions of others.

Wisdom is born of concentration.

What we need to do is simply stop for a moment, breathe, and come into awareness of precisely what is taking place—then try to act more skillfully, more appropriately, with consideration for all parties in the situation.

By being mindfully present in the moment, you can create karmic seeds of happiness.

If you train and direct your mind along paths you want it to travel, you will achieve great happiness.

Whatever you do, do it wholeheartedly, with full awareness. Even when breathing, do that wholeheartedly. It is doing by way of actively *not* doing.

Make up your mind to be happy.

Experience each moment mindfully, without attachment, striving, grasping, or involvement, but with fully involved appreciation for the essence of the moment. How great to sweep the porch, to drive down the highway, to simply sit and be yourself.

Mindfulness dramatically amplifies the probability that any activity in which you are engaged will result in an expansion of your perspective and understanding of who you are. It's a remembering, a reminding yourself to be awake.

Mindful communication means to be aware of what we are saying and to use conscious, loving speech. It also means listening deeply to the other person to hear what is being said and what is not being said. We can use these methods in any situation, anytime, wherever we are.

For mindfulness, you need nonjudging, patience, a beginner's mind, trust, nonstriving, acceptance, and letting go.

You are what you think. Pain will follow bad thoughts as certain as happiness will follow good ones.

You can live each moment free from the past and the future if you stay highly alert.

Keep your attention inside, and at the same time look around and allow yourself to be aware of the wonders that surround you.

When we attain a clarity of vision, we are able to marvel at the simple things in life that we ordinarily pass over.

Internal quiet is the only real solitude, anyway, and it is possible to find it in any situation. If you can get quiet in the middle of chaos, you can get quiet anywhere.

With mindfulness, you treasure your happiness and can make it last longer.

We can unlock the potential for happiness and satisfaction that lies within each of us by becoming aware of our mental processes and then applying discriminating wisdom to all our actions of body, speech, and mind.

Do every little thing with mindful awareness, and you will be living Zen.

Mindfulness does the job of massaging your internal formations, your blocks of suffering.

The more we deliberately bring up enjoyable states of mind, the more interesting it becomes, and the better we get at it. Every day, every moment, we can cultivate unbounded loving-kindness, sympathetic joy, deep compassion, and profound equanimity.

Mindfulness training: *Aware of the suffering caused by unmindful speech and the inability to listen to others, I am committed to cultivate loving speech and deep listening in order to bring joy and happiness to others and relieve others of their suffering. Knowing that words can create happiness or suffering, I am committed to learn to speak truthfully, with words that inspire self-confidence, joy, and hope. I am determined not to spread news that I do not know to be certain and not to criticize or condemn things of which I am not sure. I will refrain from uttering words that can cause division or discord, or that can cause the family or community to break. I will make all efforts to reconcile and resolve all conflicts, however small.*

You are not your thoughts.

Make a great effort to establish mindfulness and to calm the body and the mind so that both are firm and resolved.

Freedom from thought does not mean no thoughts. It means that thoughts come and go freely. We don't latch onto them.

Keep yourself as open and accepting as possible.

Sometimes the best way to feel your feeling or think your thoughts is to give yourself the gift of silence. Listen to the silence. Then your feelings and thoughts have a space to live in for a while.

Direct awareness and continuity of experience give our life purpose and meaning.

If you master the mind, you will have mastery over body and speech. This is done through constant awareness of all your thoughts and actions.

The mind is all the basic equipment you need to achieve happiness.

Examining my mental continuum throughout all my actions, as soon as a delusion develops whereby I or others would act inappropriately, may I firmly face it and avert it.

BUDDHA

Mindfulness gives us the time we need to prevent and overcome negative patterns of thought and behavior and so cultivate and maintain positive patterns. It gets us to turn off the automatic pilot and helps us take charge of our thoughts, words, and deeds.

The purpose of mindfulness is to open the wisdom eye, because insight into the true nature of reality is the ultimate secret of lasting peace and happiness.

Positive thoughts and feelings are health-enhancing. Feeling trust and seeing the basic goodness in others and ourselves has healing power. Seeing crises and threats as challenges and opportunities allows us to heal.

If you think that you are happy, that is enough to be happy.

If we wish to protect ourselves from suffering, either we can try to change the whole world—or we can change our mind.
GESHE KELSANG GYATSO

Practice mindful consumption. Vow to ingest only items that preserve peace, well-being, and joy in your body and in your consciousness.

With mindfulness and awareness, we pry our mind away from fantasies, chatter, and subtle whispers of thoughts. We place it here and now.

When the mind is not scattered, there is a feeling of completeness and nonfragmentation, which brings about a happiness that is completely different from the pleasure we conventionally experience.

Before you speak or act, stop for a moment and think: Are you about to be helpful or harmful? Are you about to be skillful or unskillful? Are you about to be selfless or selfish? Are your words and actions filled with loving-kindness and *bodhicitta*? Think kindly, speak gently and clearly: which thoughts do you sincerely want to express?

If you are able to maintain continuous mindfulness, nothing will upset you. You will not become angry or agitated. You can be patient no matter what anyone says or does. You can stay peaceful and happy. An unwholesome or negative state of mind cannot arise at the same moment as a moment of mindfulness.

Tranquility is the condition in which our mind has settled and is happy to be present with whatever is happening.

Maintain an awareness of the preciousness of human life.

264

To live means to be aware, joyously, drunkenly, serenely, divinely aware.
HENRY MILLER

The best way to support children in developing mindfulness is for us to live mindfully.

Happiness doesn't depend on the actual number of blessings we manage to scratch from life, only our attitude toward them.
ALEXANDER SOLZHENITSYN

Think happy thoughts.

Let your mind become clear, like a still pond.

Freeing the mind to do its dance without interference and control leads to acceptance of what is. That is the freedom that leads to true happiness.

Seek happiness in solitude and not in material pleasures.

Thinking can make us happy or miserable.

266

Mindfulness has the flavor of calm receptivity; it reminds us of that powerful moment of presence before the words begin to flow.

You are in charge of what enters your mind.

Mindfulness simply knows what is happening—it does not judge, does not try to push away, does not cling.

Notice all the layers of sound. Notice happy sounds.

Quiet is truly inside you.

Cultivating mindfulness teaches us to calm down enough to enter and dwell in states of deep relaxation.

When you practice mindful breathing, it is not difficult to be there for the people you love.

Practicing mindfulness helps us learn to appreciate the well-being that is already there. With mindfulness, we treasure our happiness and can make it last longer.

Purity of view is a gateway to greater insight and even deeper levels of happiness. The momentum of mindfulness becomes so strong that the perception of phenomena arising and passing away becomes crystal clear. Concentration and awareness are effortless. The mind becomes luminous. This point in the practice is called Vipassana happiness. It is a very happy time in our meditation. The joy of it far exceeds the happiness of concentration or of sense pleasures, because we experience such precise, clear insight into the nature of things. It's our first taste of coming home. We feel tremendous rapture and overwhelming gratitude: after all the work we've done, we're finally reaping a great reward.

JOSEPH GOLDSTEIN

Third mindfulness training: *Aware of the suffering caused by sexual misconduct, I am committed to cultivate responsibility and learn ways to protect the safety and integrity of individuals, couples, family, and society. I am determined not to engage in sexual relations without love and a long-term commitment. To preserve the happiness of myself and others, I am determined to respect my commitments and the commitments of others. I will do everything in my power to protect children from sexual abuse and to prevent couples and families from being broken by sexual misconduct.*

Have your thoughts, but don't mistake them for who you are.

Mindfulness is the foundation of happiness.

Mindfulness provides a simple but powerful route for getting ourselves unstuck, back in touch with our wisdom and vitality.

Become mindful of everything you think and learn to change it from unwholesome to wholesome.

Make any transition
a conscious one.

Mindfulness creates a space for
us to dip into our hearts and
come back up with a pearl of
kindness.

Happiness is something that you
are, and it comes from the way
you think.

Your faith in the practices
of mindfulness, in the unerring
rightness of what this moment
offers you, will help you walk
through many doors that
otherwise might be closed
to you.

The secret to an awakened life is to be completely, deeply still; expansive; and present in the heart of whatever you are doing.

If you expect your life to be up and down, your mind will be much more peaceful.

When we work with attention and joy, genuine satisfaction will be our pay.

Simply by being conscious of the present moment so we can ground ourselves in it, we relax our sense of self and begin to tune in to reality as it is.

You can remain centered in a moment of stress and recognize both the stressfulness and your impulses to react. Allow yourself to feel threatened or fearful or angry or hurt or tense. Being conscious in the present, you can recognize these as thoughts, feelings, sensations.

During commercials, hit mute and take some mindful breaths.

Just being aware of the mind that thinks it knows all the time is a major step toward learning to see through your opinions and perceive things as they actually are.

Listen to a sound, from beginning to end.

Happiness is also a way of interpreting the world, since while it may be difficult to change the world, it is always possible to change the way we look at it.

Each mindful meal, each cup of tea, can make you feel better. Touch the wonders of life within and around you. Allow the beautiful and healing elements to penetrate you.

The practice is to smile as soon as we wake up, recognizing this day as an opportunity for practicing.

To be mindful and honest makes our minds quieter and more open, our hearts happier and more peaceful.

Try to be mindful and let things take their natural course.
Then your mind will become still in any surroundings, like a still forest
pool. All kinds of wonderful animals will come to drink at the pool,
and you will clearly see the nature of all things. You will see many
strange and wonderful things come and go, but you will be still.
This is the happiness of the Buddha.

You can cultivate a mind that neither clings nor rejects, and thereby
alter the way in which you experience time and yourself.

The time you spend doing everyday tasks is precious.
It is a time for being alive. When you practice mindful living,
peace will bloom during your daily activities.

Second mindfulness training: Aware of suffering created by attachment
to views and wrong perceptions, we are determined to avoid being
narrow-minded and bound to present views. We shall learn and
practice nonattachment from views in order to be open to others'
insights and experiences. We are aware that the knowledge we
presently possess is not changeless, absolute truth. Truth is found in
life, and we will observe life within and around us in every moment,
ready to learn throughout our lives.

Learn a natural quietness of mind and openness of heart.

Mindfulness can help you understand the Four Noble Truths and the eight steps of the path to happiness.

When the mind is soft and nongrasping, we don't get caught up in the melodramas that cause such pain to ourselves and to others.

Each footstep should be regarded as a unique event in itself.

We learn as we become able to live fully in the moment,
rather than being lost in dreams, plans, memories, and commentaries
of the thinking mind. There is a big difference between drinking a cup
of tea while being there completely and drinking a cup of tea while
thinking about five other things. There is a big difference between
taking a walk in the woods and really being there—and taking a walk
while planning dinner or imagining the stories you will have about your
walk. It is only by being fully in the moment that the fundamental
questions of the heart can be answered.

Really do what you are doing.
Be awake and alive as you do it,
mindful of the tendency to go on autopilot.

Choiceless awareness is simply being receptive to whatever unfolds in each moment.

When we pay full attention to our world, we are happier and more effective.

The practices of mindfulness and loving-kindness help us to understand that all things deserve care—that when we relate to all things with kindness, we are relating to ourselves with kindness.

Have an ease and openness of mind that receives with interest every kind of circumstances—asking yourself what you can learn from each experience.

Let the discerning person guard his mind, so difficult to detect and extremely subtle, wandering wherever it desires. A guarded mind brings happiness.

BUDDHA

Recognize that positive thinking is a powerful force in achieving your goals.

Drink a cup of tea. Don't think about drinking a cup of it—just drink it. Taste it. Feel it. Enjoy it. That is experience beyond thought.

Live with a sense of urgency and complete awareness.

The ability to be in the present moment is a major component of mental wellness.
ABRAHAM MASLOW

Follow the unfolding of daily events as the activity of the enlightened ones.

Concentrate and nurture your mind.

Mindful awareness rather than merely thinking can lead us to wisdom and to a happiness based on what is true.

Pay as exquisite attention as possible to your every thought and activity from moment to moment. It helps you to stop and ultimately becomes a different and profound way of life.

The better your mind gets at totally immersing itself in what you are doing, the less you will be plagued by distractions, desires, and fragmentation—and the more satisfying your daily existence will become.

When engaged in activity, keep your attention on your breath.

Bring attention to all the things you have taken for granted and never noticed.

The practice of mindfulness is simply to bring awareness into each moment of our lives.

Happiness comes from within our own minds through the use of mindfulness—to clear away greed, hatred, and delusion.

The sense of well-being that comes with repeatedly being able to bring your mind to a state of stillness begins to permeate everything else in your life.

If you are reading, try stopping every half hour. Close your eyes for a minute or so and bring your attention back to your breath.

The root of happiness is in our minds. Outer circumstances are just adverse or favorable.

Relating to the present moment with joy is a choice we can make.

Everything you need to live mindfully and completely is already within you.

Mindfulness is willingness to make peace with all moments and all things.

Use nonjudgmental, meditative awareness to help open up your mind and dance with ideas instead of fixating on them.

Every wakeful step, every mindful act, is the path.

Genuine happiness is living in a simple, direct way, without cluttering up the mind with wanting things, hating things, judging, taking too much, worrying, or doubting.

Constant mindfulness brings tranquility and insight so you can sustain wisdom even in the midst of ordinary activities and distractions.

Contemplating your food for a few seconds before eating, and eating in mindfulness, can bring you much happiness. To aid mindfulness during meals, you may like to eat silently from time to time. Turn off the talking to enjoy the food.

Fourth mindfulness training: *Aware of the suffering caused by unmindful speech and the inability to listen to others, I am committed to cultivate loving speech and deep listening in order to bring joy and happiness to others and relieve others of their suffering. Knowing that words can create happiness or suffering, I am committed to learn to speak truthfully, with words that inspire self-confidence, joy, and hope. I am determined not to spread news that I do not know to be certain and not to criticize or condemn things of which I am not sure. I will refrain from uttering words that can cause division or discord, or that can cause the family or community to break. I will make all efforts to reconcile and resolve all conflicts, however small.*

Let yourself have your feelings. Let the feelings flow through you. Then let them end. Let yourself see to the other side of them.

Bring awareness to your body. When you sit, know you are sitting. When you eat, know you are eating. When you walk, feel the sensations of the body walking.

If you do something, you should be very observant, careful, alert. Put the dough in the oven and watch it rise.

When the mind is still, you can hear the silence and let it guide you.

Overcoming Obstacles

On our path of living, we deal with
many obstacles: ignorance, craving
or desire, clinging or attachment,
and the inherent suffering of life—
aging, sickness, and death. We
create many of these troubles for
ourselves, so it is important to
work on recognizing this and also
learn to let go of the past *and* the
future. This is done by staying
mindful in the moment and
cultivating right understanding.
The seeds you plant determine
what will grow.

Three reasons for dissatisfaction and unhappiness: ignorance of the truth, attachment, aversion.

We take for permanent that which is ephemeral and for happiness that which is but a source of suffering: the desire for wealth, for power, for fame, and for nagging pleasure.

Have a repentant tongue—most bad karma is created by speech. Watch your tongue carefully, and be sure that it is always used with compassion and intelligence.

Wealth is the number of things one can do without.

He who seeks happiness by hurting those who seek happiness will never find happiness.

.

Every minute you are angry, you lose sixty seconds of happiness.
RALPH WALDO EMERSON

Desirelessness is nirvanic peace. Relinquishing clinging and attachment does ultimately pay off.

Look for the rainbow when it rains.

We always try to accumulate more and more, thinking that these things are essential for our existence. In fact, they may be obstacles that prevent us from being happy. Release these things and become a free person. Release them so you can be truly happy.

Happiness is being free from desires.

See the unfavorable environment and unhappiness of an angry person and breathe in. Understand the causes of this unhappiness and breathe out.

We don't need anything outside ourselves to be happy; attachment will not lead to happiness.

Attachment will never procure you a happy rebirth; it kills the life of liberation.

How can you quarrel—knowing that life is as fleeting as a rainbow, a flash of lightning, a star at dawn?

No matter how judgmental, blaming, punishing, bitter, or cynical someone is toward you—use your compassion and it will not affect you. It is the antidote.

Keep looking at a problem nonjudgmentally, and practice will teach you what you need to know next.

Every time you smile away your irritation and anger, you achieve a victory for yourself and humanity.

A specific way of dealing with ill will when it is too overpowering is to generate loving thoughts: wishing happiness and love to all beings everywhere, to individual people you feel very kindly toward, and finally to the specific person you may be angry at—offering loving thoughts, even though it may be difficult.

When we get angry about anything at all, first remember that you are the owner of your karma. Don't condemn yourself. Then change the reaction. Substitute loving-kindness.

A conditional happiness dependent on any specific circumstances always leads to suffering.

Your trials did not come to punish you, but to awaken you— to make you realize that you are part of Spirit and that just behind the spark of your life is the flame of infinity.

One who overcomes anger is loved by all and is delightful—his mind is calm, his face is pure, and he is trusted by everyone.

When you are suffering, look deeply at your situation and find the conditions for happiness that are already there, already available.

There is no lasting peace through addiction or attachment; will a bag of M&M's bring happiness?

It is often our very idea of happiness that prevents us from being happy.

When you feel pain, instead of immediately adding suffering, just note it without interpretation.

Part of Zen is learning to break those old bad habits that aren't doing you any good. You'll perceive *dukkha*, but it won't bother you, drive you up the wall, or make you miserable. You'll say *There it is* and let it go.

No matter how difficult the past, you can always begin again today.

The Buddha's point about happiness is very similar. As long as we continue trying to eliminate all displeasure and preserve only pleasure for a prolonged sense of well-being, no lasting happiness is possible. Rage, envy, and the desire for revenge will always interfere. Real life and its complications inevitably trickle in.

MARK EPSTEIN

Realize that anger is useless. It makes you unhappy. It makes a groove in the mind so that anger arises more and more easily.

Happy indeed are we who
live without possessions.
Let us feed on happiness,
like the radiant gods
(who feed on spiritual bliss).

DHAMMAPADA

Renounce the habitual grasping, unhappy mind.

We create much optional suffering through the stories we tell ourselves about what we believe will bring us happiness.

Suffering is caused by desire. Desire is wanting something you don't have, wishing something were some way it isn't, or being otherwise generally dissatisfied with the way things are, in a belief that things would be better, you would be happier, life would be sweeter if only this were the case, if only that would happen, if only something were different than the way it is now.

There is no point to making much ado about nothing.

Our true enemies are the mental poisons of ignorance, hatred, desire, jealousy, and pride. They are the only things capable of destroying our happiness.

There is nothing clever about not being happy.

When unpleasant things arise or you don't get what you want, reflect that all things are impermanent and that, sooner or later, your suffering will change.

Every mind moment that is free of greed, hatred, and delusion has a certain purifying force in the flow of consciousness.

Enjoy the happiness of calming your desires.

Make yourself such that you can tolerate anything. Let yourself be impervious to suffering.

Though outer events may be difficult, the key to our happiness is how our mind responds to them.

Laughter makes us grow more enlightened. It shrinks the exaggerated seriousness of our problems by making us relax our fixation on them.

Confront challenges with inner strength and courage.

People who create problems for us provide us with a good opportunity to practice tolerance and patience.

Fewer complexities and attachments allow us to live more happily and contentedly.

If we are using strong negative emotions to get what we want and what we want is happiness, it is never going to work.

Contemplate the damage from anger to self and others, and breathe in. See that anger burns and destroys happiness, and breathe out.

If we cannot be happy in spite of our difficulties, what good is our spiritual practice?

In conflict, be fair and generous.

Use times of suffering or unhappiness as opportunities to pay particular attention.

Free the mind to do its dance without interference and control; this leads to acceptance of what is, the freedom that leads to true happiness.

If you don't attach to your feelings, they won't hang around. Enter and experience your pain, rather than try to distract yourself from it.

Laugh when you let yourself get caught up in something small.

No matter how hectic or troublesome things appear, we need only to turn inward to find peace. In the eye of a storm there is stillness.

If we practice nonaggression when we feel irritated with our spouse, instead of aggravating the situation with anger, we can resolve our differences peacefully and maintain harmony.

When we can look into the face of suffering without flinching, we will also be able to recognize true happiness.

The best remedy for those who are afraid, lonely, or unhappy is to go outside, somewhere where they can be quiet, alone with the heavens, nature, and God. Because only then does one feel that all is as it should be.

ANNE FRANK

Desires create suffering, whether they make you happy or sad. Use your practice to go beyond them.

Being free of false identifications is like going to a huge park and standing in the middle of a wide-open field: clear air, unobstructed views and movement, and infinite potential.

If you stay unconscious, true happiness will prove elusive.

Let go of anger with gentleness.

Clinging to anything makes us unhappy.

The more we let go of craving, the greater our sense of happiness.

Our resentment of others fails to transfer even a shred of their happiness to us, but succeeds in choking our minds with negativity. So stop—if you want to be free.

By not knowing the basic interdependent nature of reality and by not recognizing the consequences of our actions, we set off on a course that produces the unhappy results brought by attachment and aversion.

Happy indeed we live, friendly amid the hostile! Amid hostile people we dwell free from hatred.
BUDDHA

If a behavior or way of thinking does not have a positive payoff of making your life happy, it can and should be changed.

In times of need, one should rise to the occasion and fight bravely for what is right.
DALAI LAMA

When something bad or embarrassing happens that is relatively minor, try to laugh and let the incident go as soon as possible, getting on with life and being determined not to let what happened affect you adversely.

Regard difficulties as opportunities to learn something.

Remove the suffering and you get happiness.

By not polluting the world with worries and conflict, you are instantly doing the world a great service.

Wise avoidance is the willingness to see but unwillingness to engage in pathways of suffering.

For the uncontrolled there is no wisdom. For the uncontrolled there is no concentration, and for him without concentration, there is no peace. And for the unpeaceful, how can there ever be happiness?

BHAGAVAD GITA

True renunciation involves rejecting any thought, intention, word, or action that causes suffering to ourselves and others.

In difficult circumstances, the most skillful thing you can do is to find time and space to be alone and to practice nonaction until negative feelings subside.

Why cling to the pain and the wrongs of yesterday? Why hold on to the very things that keep you from hope and love?

BUDDHA

We do not recognize the empty nature of words, and yet we fixate on them as if they were real. Our happy and unhappy reactions to them are both a sign that we believe in the reality of words.

Try to abandon actions that are simply something to do and that do not lead toward happiness.

Do not think that because you are suffering you can speak harshly, retaliate, or punish others. Breathe in and remember your Buddha nature, your capacity for calm and compassion.

By releasing the beliefs and concepts that hold solid your sense of self, you soften the ground of basic goodness so that love and compassion can break through.

Realize: *This situation is not a problem. I am not suffering. I am happy*.

What cowardice it is to be dismayed by the happiness of others and devastated by their good fortune.

We are learning how to work with all our reactions, emotional and physical, so that we may be less controlled by them, and see more clearly what we should do and how we might respond effectively.

Those desiring to escape from suffering hasten right toward it. With the very desire for happiness, out of delusion they destroy their own happiness as if it were an enemy.

SHANTIDEVA

There is only one way to happiness and that is to cease worrying about things that are beyond the power of our will.
EPICTETUS

Clean up your own room.

Freedom from craving is an important practice. Look deeply into the nature of what you think will bring you happiness and see whether it is, in fact, causing others to suffer.

The drama of the world loses its grip on you when you stop believing that its characters and situations are permanent or truly threatening. The urgency dissolves and you calmly go from encounter to encounter, enjoying every moment to its fullest, without fear. Life becomes peaceful, fluid, easy, and beautiful.

Everything can be perfect. Bad things happen to everyone and nobody likes them. How you handle those bad things is what causes your suffering, not the bad thing itself. Attaching to bad things, trying to control them, or letting them control you—these are the attitudes that cause suffering.

When others out of jealousy harm me or insult me, may I take defeat on myself and offer them the victory.

BUDDHA

Envy and jealousy stem from the fundamental inability to rejoice at someone else's happiness or success.

You can go through your problems and expose them to acceptance instead of denying their existence. The problems dissolve. Like exposing a snowflake to a furnace, problems do not stand a chance against true love.

How have we lived recently that has contributed to our suffering? We need to recognize and identify the nutrients we ingest, and observe: *When I think like this, speak like that, listen like this, or act like that, my suffering increases*. We tend to blame others for our unhappiness.

Seek happiness in the senses, indulge in food and sleep, and you too will be uprooted.

Facing the truth of dissatisfaction helps us recognize true happiness.

Healing begins with caring.

Finding the Path to Happiness

Each step along the Buddha's path to happiness requires practicing mindfulness until it becomes part of your daily life. Mindfulness is a way of training yourself to become aware of things as they really are. With mindfulness as your key, you progress through the eight steps on the path to happiness explained by the Buddha—a gentle, gradual training to end suffering.

The eight steps of the Buddha's path bring peace and happiness. They are Skillful Understanding, Skillful Thinking, Skillful Speech, Skillful Action, Skillful Livelihood, Skillful Effort, Skillful Mindfulness, and Skillful Concentration.

Recognize that all created things pass and what matters is not how much we collect or what we make or do, but how well we live this short dance and how well we learn to love.

On the strength of your resolve, you discover true happiness.

Skillful Effort has four parts: preventing negative states of mind, overcoming negative states of mind, cultivating positive states of mind, and maintaining positive states of mind.

There is no way to happiness—happiness *is* the way.
BUDDHA

Make your thoughts still, your words still; make work into stillness.

It is not possible to live happily if one does not lead a beautiful, righteous, and wise life, or to lead a beautiful, righteous, and wise life if one is not happy.
EPICURUS

Make happiness a factor in decision making.

Whenever I associate with others, may I view myself as the lowest of all; and with a perfect intention, may I cherish others as supreme.

BUDDHA

Repeat to yourself what you know of the teachings of the Buddha or your understanding of what brings about your happiness.

Unwrap the precious Buddha, the one wrapped up inside you.

Perfect happiness is the absence of the striving for happiness; perfect renown is the absence of concern for renown.

CHUANG-TSE

The Three Refuges involve strengthening our intentions to let go of suffering and to cultivate happiness. Bring your palms together with your fingers pointing to your chin at the level of your heart. Spend a few moments considering your intentions, then take the refuges formally: *I take refuge in the Buddha. I take refuge in the Dharma. I take refuge in the Sangha.* You can do this at any time during the day or at the beginning of another meditation practice.

For an exam: Visualize yourself feeling very much at ease about the test and speaking or writing the answers very confidently. You are relaxed and happy, speaking or writing smoothly and comfortably. At the end, see yourself feeling extremely pleased with what you have done and confident that you are going to pass. Keep this image in your mind as long as possible. Reinforce the visualization by repeating an affirmation like *I can handle this* or *I am very confident.*

In any sort of Buddhism, it seems beyond question
that Buddhahood is a synonym for supreme happiness.
To state my thesis succinctly, from the Buddhist perspective
enlightenment is happiness. So naturally a Buddha smiles.
ROBERT THURMAN

Embracing death brings with it deep and lasting happiness based on
the acceptance of life and its cycles. When you look into your own eyes,
you will see a soul instead of just desire and drama. You become much
freer and happier.

While chasing his mythical happiness of the future, man has no time to enjoy the present moment.

Happiness is a universal phenomenon. Trees and animals and birds and plants are happy. The whole of existence is happy except for man. Being miserable is specific to man. Misery makes you special, but there is nothing special about happiness because it is a universal phenomenon.

Analyze your life closely. If you do, you will eventually find it difficult to misuse your life by seeking money or things as the path to happiness.

Nirvana is the state of being where there is no grasping, no desire for things to be different from the way they are.

Practicing the Dharma is indispensable. But to practice it, it is essential that a person know what it is. So learning is the first thing to do. The Way is immense; we cannot learn all about it. However, the more we learn and practice it, the greater our happiness becomes.

There is a sense of pleasure and relief every time we let go.

Speech creates an environment that either contributes to happiness or destroys it.

When you stop wanting, then you are happy. How can that be? It just is.

321

Although Bertha Young was thirty she still had moments like this when she wanted to run instead of walk, to take dancing steps on and off the pavement, to bowl a hoop, to throw something up in the air and catch it again, or to stand still and laugh at—nothing—at nothing, simply. What can you do if you are thirty and, turning the corner of your own street, you are overcome, suddenly by a feeling of bliss—absolute bliss!—as though you'd suddenly swallowed a bright piece of that late afternoon sun and it burned in your bosom, sending out a little shower of sparks into every particle, into every finger and toe?

Surrender to the perfect mystery and accept each moment as perfect and essential for your evolution. It is that simple.

You cannot overdo these things: refining your speech, practicing generosity and loving-kindness, being present.

Joyful effort is trying hard and finding pleasure in the exertion—and is a major contributor to happiness.

Other things being equal, a life filled with complex flow activities is more worth living than one spent consuming passive entertainment.
MIHALY CSIKSZENTMIHALYI

Happiness is a process, not a destination. So work as if you do not need money. Love as if you have never been hurt. Dance as though no one is watching.

323

Happiness comes not from reaching out but from letting go and opening in the moment to what is true.

If you see a greater pleasure that comes from forsaking a lesser pleasure, you should be willing to do so.
There's always a tradeoff.

The more we let go, the lighter the mind becomes.

With the Bodhisattva vow, you aspire to use your life to awaken in order to help all beings do the same.

Don't plan it; live it.

Those who seek happiness in pleasure, wealth, glory, power, and heroics are as naïve as the child who tries to catch a rainbow and wear it as a coat.

The middle path is to be aware of how things are happening, to be wakeful and balanced, not clingy, not condemning, not identifying things with I or self.

A Buddha is someone who lives in peace, joy, and freedom, neither afraid of nor attached to anything.

Be interested in doing this very simple thing in the moment.

Even a happy life cannot be without a measure of darkness, and the word happiness would lose its meaning if it were not balanced by sadness.

CARL JUNG

Write the words *What Am I Doing?* on a piece of paper and hang it where you will see it often. It will help you release your thinking about the past or the future and return to the present moment.

Looking for lasting happiness outside yourself is useless; it is like expecting to get in shape by watching others exercise.

Surrender everything—your body, your life, your inner self—and you will experience peace, ease, nondoing, and inexpressible happiness.
YUAN-WU

Identify your happy colors—wear them and decorate with them.

Right mindfulness is whatever one is doing to be inwardly aware of the physical body. Recognize that you are not the body, and you will be free of everything.

It is by studying little things that we attain the great art of having as little misery and as much happiness as possible.
SAMUEL JOHNSON

Happiness does not come automatically.
It is not a gift that good fortune bestows on us and
a reversal of fortune takes back. It depends on us alone.
One does not become happy overnight, but with patient labor, day
after day. Happiness is constructed, and that requires effort and time.
In order to become happy, we have to learn how to change ourselves.

Helen Keller said that true happiness is attained through fidelity to a
worthy purpose.

The middle path emphasizes simplicity and nonviolence.

Sit back and relax into the richness of what is.

Realize that complete satisfaction does not exist and, instead, set your sights on being generally satisfied and generally happy.

Without looking out your window you can know the way of heaven.
GEORGE HARRISON

329

Learn to make peace with whatever is present.

Having an image of the Buddha or Dalai Lama in your home or office is inspiring.

On its own, no amount of technological development can lead to lasting happiness. What is almost always missing is a corresponding inner development.
DALAI LAMA

Each moment that we live without clinging or aversion, we live in freedom.

Pursue happiness in every corner of your life.

Remember three essentials for happiness: something to do, someone to love, something to hope for.

Be happy with what you have while working for what you want.

You must also use loving speech. We have to have the capacity to say things calmly. Don't get irritated too easily. Don't let sour or bitter speech leave your mouth. Get back a capacity for speaking with kindness.

The Second Noble Truth is that suffering is caused by craving and aversion. We will suffer if we expect other people to conform to our expectation, if we want others to like us, if we do not get something we want, and so on. In other words, getting what you want does not guarantee happiness. Rather than constantly struggling to get what you want, try to modify your wanting. Wanting deprives us of contentment and happiness. A lifetime of wanting and craving, and especially the craving to continue to exist, creates a powerful energy that causes the individual to be born. So craving leads to physical suffering because it causes us to be reborn.

Work with the precepts, live with contentment and simplicity that does not exploit other people.

True freedom requires wisdom. Wisdom cuts through ignorance. Wisdom can be acquired only through the power of concentration. The stabilized mind of concentration depends on freeing ourselves from the pull of negative addictions.

Others may know pleasure, but pleasure is not happiness.
MUHAMMAD ALI

Awareness, insight, and health ripen on their own if we are willing to pay attention in the moment and remember that we have only moments to live.

Right concentration is to be free of desire and not allow the torment of the mind to have any effect. Being in that secluded place where there is true awareness of joy and happiness is concentration.

Be sure your mind is engaged
before putting your mouth
into gear.

Slow down and see where
you are going.

The ancient Greek definition of
happiness was the full use of
your powers along lines of
excellence.
JOHN F. KENNEDY

Remove the notions of self,
person, living being,
and life span if you want to
be free and happy.

Flow with whatever may happen and let your mind be free.

A Bodhisattva who accepts suffering courageously will always be happy.
DHARMARAKSHITA

Does anyone think, in the end, *I wish I had worked more?*

Try as much as possible to be wholly alive, with all your might, and when you laugh, laugh like hell and when you get angry, get good and angry. Try to be alive. You will be dead soon enough.

We mistake pleasure for happiness even though we know pleasure doesn't make us happy. Pleasure is pleasure, a temporary gratification of desire. Happiness is a deeper satisfaction, a feeling of wholeness, of non-neediness.

Happiness comes when your work and words are of benefit to yourself and others.
BUDDHA

Moderation is the only way to find true balance and the best way to live fully and with mindful awareness.

With understanding, all things become possible.

Life and happiness are driven from the inside out.

Furthermore, through all these method practices, together with a mind that is undefiled by stains of conceptions of the eight extremes and that sees all phenomena as illusory, may I be released from the bondage of mistaken appearance and conceptions.

BUDDHA

Wherever you see practices leading to happiness, always exert effort in them.

Seize today, and put as little trust as you can in the morrow.

HORACE

Give yourself to the journey.

Know that joy is unaffected by outer circumstance, and joy will be yours forever.

To be nobody but yourself in a world which is doing its best to make you everybody else, means to fight the hardest human battle ever and to never stop fighting.
E. E. CUMMINGS

Right thought is thinking kindly and refuses to engage in cruel, mean, covetous, or other nasty thoughts.
What you think is what you are.

Let go of the need to know so much. Trust in simplicity and love.

Decide you want a happy ending and try to make your dream a reality.

Whenever I see unfortunate beings oppressed by evil and violent suffering, may I cherish them as if I had found a rare and precious treasure.

BUDDHA

Happiness is not in our circumstances, but in ourselves. It is not something we see, like a rainbow, or feel, like the heat of a fire. Happiness is something we are.

Words can cause suffering, so I vow to speak only with kindness and love and to listen deeply, never speaking words that could cause division and discord but working to avoid or resolve conflict. Parents who lie, speak in anger, criticize, or belittle others in front of their children or to their children teach their kids that words are weapons to be used against others. Parents who use words carefully, deliberately, and in a way that supports and upholds life and happiness teach kids that language can be a powerful instrument of compassion and strength.

Happiness isn't about getting something in the future. Happiness is the capacity to open the heart and eyes and spirit and be where we are and find happiness in the midst of it. Even in the place of difficulty, there is a kind of happiness that comes if we've been compassionate, that can help us through it. So it's different than pleasure, and it's different than chasing after something.

JACK KORNFIELD

Any particular manifestation of Buddha is thus a kind of living doorway to each individual's own happiness, a mirror, to that individual, of the reality that must be understood for that individual to realize their own wisdom, freedom from suffering, immortality, and supreme happiness.

ROBERT THURMAN

Human happiness has no perfect security but freedom; freedom none but virtue; virtue none but knowledge.

Start every day a little happier.

If you cling to nothing, you can handle anything.

Satisfying our desires does not bring authentic happiness, merely temporary gratification. We can conclude that satisfying our desires does not cause real, lasting happiness. Real, lasting happiness arises from eliminating desire for the things we like and aversion to things we don't like. It is not bad or wrong to want or enjoy good things. We do need to realize that desire itself is the obstacle to finding true happiness.

There is happiness in life, happiness in friendship, happiness of a family, happiness in a healthy body and mind, …but when one loses them, there is suffering.

BUDDHA

If you continue searching for happiness where it cannot be found, there is suffering.

Seeking happiness outside ourselves is like waiting for sunshine in a cave facing north.
TIBETAN SAYING

Voluntary simplicity helps us experience a greater and greater peace.

Remember, work is the necessary condition of happiness—favorite and free work and also the physical work that arouses your appetite.

Pleasure is only the shadow of
happiness.
HINDU PROVERB

Choose happiness.

Pleasure is the happiness of
madmen, while happiness is the
pleasure of sages.

Stay happy and present and
you'll have no reason to
remember or repeat the past.

The basis of Right Action is to do everything in mindfulness.

Nirvana is the freedom from attachments to thoughts, feelings, and desires—and a complete and total absorption in the present moment.

Cultivating balance in your life can help you get in touch with your inner self. Every day—think a little, feel a little, move a little, rest a little, eat a little, drink a little, sleep a little, and meditate a little. Don't let any one activity dominate and you will cultivate an inner equilibrium and contentment.

Be guided by principles instead of reacting to momentary conditions or temporary circumstances.

What the Buddha taught on so many levels was how to be happy. If we want the happiness of sense delights, there are causes and conditions, namely, purity of conduct. If we want the happiness of stillness, of peace, we need to develop concentration—one-pointedness of mind. If we want the happiness of insight, we need to develop purity of view, purity of understanding through strengthening mindfulness. If we want to experience the happiness of different stages of insight, all the way through equanimity, we need to continue building the momentum of mindfulness and the other factors of enlightenment. And if we want the highest happiness, the happiness of nibbana, we simply need to walk this path to the end. And when we aim for the highest kind of happiness, we find all the others a growing part of our lives.

JOSEPH GOLDSTEIN

A man is happy so long as he
choose to be happy.
ALEXANDER SOLZHENITSYN

The man who is born
with a talent that he is meant
to use finds his greatest
happiness in using it.
GOETHE

Glorious is it to see the Noble
Ones; their company at all times
brings happiness; by not seeing
the spiritually ignorant, one will
always be happy.
DHAMMAPADA

Become conscious of all the
options for increasing the
happiness of your immediate
surroundings.

If there is a way to free ourselves from suffering, we must use every moment to find it. Only a fool wants to go on suffering.
SEVENTH DALAI LAMA

If you have to eat at McDonald's, order a Happy Meal.

One of the Buddhist teachings is that wealth does not guarantee happiness, and also wealth is impermanent. The people of every country suffer, whether rich or poor, but those who understand Buddhist teachings can find true happiness.

Joyful effort encourages you to keep trying when you feel weak and inadequate. Joyful effort creates the cause that results in feeling happy. Joyful effort gives you the courage to live life positively and well, and the humility to keep learning from the lessons life throws at you.

Six Perfections: Generosity: giving, yielding, unconditional love, open hand, mind, heart. Virtue: ethics, honesty, morality, integrity, helping others. Patience: tolerance, forbearance, acceptance, forgiveness. Effort: energy, diligence, courage, enthusiasm, endurance. Meditation: concentration, focus, self-inquiry, reflection, mindfulness. Wisdom: discernment, sagacity, sanity, centeredness, understanding.

It is the aim of all spiritual seeking to bring us home to the understanding that we already have everything we need.

You can be happy
no matter what.

There is no lasting happiness,
lasting meal, lasting
ice cream cone.

Happy endings are extremely
unreliable. Happy nows are
reliable.

The wise man is a happy child—
full of grace, freshness,
innocence, joy; awake.

There is no happiness except that found in right action.

The first level of full concentration is marked by initial application of thought, sustained application of thought, joy, happiness, and concentration functioning in unison. It is very pleasant.

The Buddha's Great Vow to Lead All People to Happiness: *At all times I think to myself, how can I cause living beings to gain entry into the unsurpassed way and quickly acquire the body of a Buddha?*
BUDDHA

Happiness is all about milking the "sacred now."
ROBERT HOLDEN

To realize that there is nothing to hold onto that can offer lasting satisfaction, shows us there is nowhere to go and nothing to have and nothing to be (= freedom).

Allow yourself the opportunity to experience both joy and suffering. They are essential elements of mindfulness practice, just as they are of daily life.

Being free from self-importance is a state of natural simplicity in harmony with your true nature.

Success is found through the end of desire, not the gratification of it.

352

Give us, oh, give us the man who sings at his work!
He will do more in the same time, he will do it better, he will persevere
longer. One is scarcely sensible of fatigue whilst he marches to music.
The very stars are said to make harmony as they revolve in their
spheres. Wondrous is the strength of cheerfulness, altogether past
calculation its powers of endurance. Efforts, to be permanently useful,
must be uniformly joyous, a spirit all sunshine, graceful from very
gladness, beautiful because bright.

THOMAS CARLYLE

When people asked Buddha why and what he taught, he replied:
I teach because you and all beings seek happiness and try to avoid
suffering. I teach the way things are. So, what is Buddhism?
Buddha used the best description himself. During the 1,500 years the
teachings existed in India, they were called Dharma, and for the last
1,000 years in Tibet, the name was Cho. Both mean the way things are.
Understanding the way things are is the key to every happiness.

BUDDHA

It is a flaw in happiness, to see beyond our bourn. It forces us in summer skies to mourn. It spoils the singing of the nightingale.
KEATS

Live your life properly, rejoice in the happiness of now, safe in the knowledge of the future.

For the Buddha, the truth is the realm of happiness. The other shore is the realm of happiness, nirvana. Jesus also says that he is the truth, because his kingdom of heaven is the realm of happiness.

No movement or direction in dance is better or worse than another. This is a way to view all of life. See all the good and bad things that happen to you simply as movements in the dance of life.

Right Effort is that which will create the necessary conditions
for mind to be focused, allowing clarity and concentration
for completion of your task.

Right Concentration means working on achieving a one-pointed mind.
If you are doing something, concentrate wholly on what you are doing.
This can be achieved through the discipline that comes from
a great deal of meditation practice.

The Five Precepts are moral guidelines that, because they are skillful, lead to happy states. Not killing or harming living beings, not lying, not stealing, not indulging in inappropriate sexual activity, not drinking or taking drugs, mean that unhappy states are less likely to occur. To harm a living being, for example, has bad karmic consequences. It can lead to feelings of remorse and regret for what one has done. It will lead to suffering.

For a job interview or public speech: Visualize yourself walking in and exuding self-confidence. You are very relaxed and talking freely and confidently with the interviewer or the audience. The exchange between you is very positive and the interviewer or audience looks enthusiastic when you are speaking. You answer all the questions happily and with confidence. At the end, the interviewer or audience shows a lot of enthusiasm for what you have said, and you feel happy that your performance has been so impressive. Keep this image in your mind as long as possible. Reinforce the visualization by repeating an affirmation like *I can handle this* or *I am very confident.*

356

It takes a living personification of the Buddha-qualities to make our own freedom and enlightenment seem really possible, a live exemplar of the Buddha-happiness to make our own mouths water for the taste of our own real happiness. This is the real meaning of the Dalai Lama's presence. It is felt by all who meet him, through whatever medium, consciously or unconsciously.

ROBERT THURMAN

Zen teaches perfect freedom to accept or reject without compulsion or remorse. The serious practitioner will find that as his subconscious fears evaporate and his compulsive habits disappear, his built-in body wisdom will naturally select the kind and quantity of food necessary for his physical, mental, and spiritual growth.

When you awake in the morning, stretch your arms to the sky and breathe deeply. Fill your insides with the emptiness around you.

Right speech means refusing to lie, talk meanly, gossip, command everyone's attention, or inflame people. Right speech should be wise, kind, and minimal. Talk when necessary.

Speak little. When necessary, use words that are sweet.

Happiness is under your feet.

Play very hard.

Write the words *Are You Sure?* on a piece of paper and hang it where you will see it often. Wrong perceptions cause incorrect thinking and unnecessary suffering.

The Buddha taught happiness in this life, and at the same time satisfied people's hope in the next life.

Advance confidently in the direction of your dreams.

But, as the Dalai Lama always emphasizes, happiness is not a hobby, nor is it a trivial pursuit. It is a fundamental drive as basic as those of sex or aggression, but not often as legitimized in our cynical, postmodern culture. In fact, Americans are waking up to the Dalai Lama's point: Materialistic comforts by themselves have not led to lasting happiness. Having reached that conclusion, however, we do not often see another way, and retreat into our comforts, barricading ourselves from what appears to be a hostile and threatening world. Acquiring and protecting, we continue to crave a happiness that seems both deserved and out of reach.

MARK EPSTEIN

Even the theorists who categorize emotions as simply positive or negative do not propose that all the negative emotions are harmful to oneself or to others. While most theorists acknowledge that emotions can on some occasions be harmful, this is not thought to be intrinsic to any particular emotion. The goal is not to rid oneself of or transcend an emotion, not even hatred, but to regulate experience and action once an emotion is felt.

A sense of wonder and delight is present in every moment, every breath, every step of ordinary life.

Dare to live the life you have dreamed for yourself. Live the life you have imagined.

If you are happy at the expense of another person's happiness, you are forever bound.

Ask yourself: *What do I truly need to be happy?*

Right action is following the Five Precepts: nonviolence or refusal to kill purposefully; refusal to steal; control of the senses and appetites; talking sincerely and honestly; refusal to alter the mind with intoxicants.

Live simply and with purity of heart, without grasping.

Create and surround yourself with beauty.

Things don't make you whole and happy; they can divide and disorient.

Think only what is right there, what is right under your nose to do. It's such a simple thing— that's why people can't do it.

HENRY MILLER

To the moment, say, *Stay now! You are beautiful!*

Be generous with your lighting; light is happiness.

A straightforward practice of cultivating what brings happiness and renouncing what brings suffering is the path.

The purpose of practicing Buddhism is to avoid suffering and find happiness. This may make us feel that creating karma that brings happiness as the result is the best thing to do. However, Buddhism teaches us that everything is impermanent, so even if we create the causes of happiness, the resulting happiness cannot last forever. Our highest aspiration is to transcend karma on our path toward enlightenment.

A man who has reached the other shore
does not carry thoughts from the other shore.
Without hatred, he does not suffer, but is happy.
Is there anyone who does not know hatred and knows
loving-kindness alone and then suffers and is not happy?
No hatred and loving-kindness alone is nirvana.

Ask yourself: *What am I waiting for to make me happy? Why am I not happy right now?*

One must practice the things that produce happiness, since if that is present we have everything and if it is absent we do everything in order to have it.
EPICURUS

Act as though it were impossible to fail.

Put happiness, joy, and pleasure first.

365

Right thought means thinking kindly and refusing to engage in cruel, mean, covetous, or otherwise nasty thoughts. What you think is what you are.

Happiness is like a sunbeam, which the least shadow intercepts, while adversity is often like the rain of spring.
CHINESE PROVERB

It is neither wealth nor splendor, but tranquility and occupation which give happiness.
THOMAS JEFFERSON

My life has no purpose, no direction, no aim, no meaning, and yet I'm happy. I can't figure it out. What am I doing right?
CHARLIE BROWN/
CHARLES M. SCHULZ

I find ecstasy in the living;
the mere sense of living
is joy enough.
EMILY DICKINSON

Do each thing with enthusiasm.

To the Dalai Lama, the purpose
of life is to be happy.

Zen is a way of being happy.
T'AO-SHAN

367

In the Individual Vehicle, there is the happiness of Nirvana, spiritual release. The Third Holy Fact (Noble Truth) is the one that Buddha staked his life's work on, the Holy Fact of Cessation of, Freedom from, Suffering. This was his good news, his discovery that he found worth sharing with other beings. Upon realizing his own freedom, he is reported to have said, Deep, peaceful, fabrication-free, translucent, uncreated—I have discovered a Reality like elixir of immortality. Whoever I might teach about it, they won't understand; better to stay in silence in the forest! Later, when he had become more optimistic about people's ability to respond to his instructions, he sent out his mendicants to spread the word, telling them to announce that The gates of Nirvana have been opened!

ROBERT THURMAN

Every meal is our last meal, every kiss our first kiss. Then we are living our life.

Why should I complain? My mind is functioning. I have all my senses. I have access to spiritual teachings, and time and a place to meditate.

We need the insight that position, revenge, wealth, fame, or possessions are, more often than not, obstacles to our happiness. We need to cultivate the wish to be free of these things so we can enjoy the wonders of life that are always available.

He is a true seeker who lives purely and self-assured, in quietness and virtue, without harm or hurt or blame.

The type of Buddhist practices that I talk about in *The Art of Happiness* have to do with reconditioning one's way of thinking and one's outlook, and one's perception and how one relates to people…. That type of thing, any Westerner can practice at any time.

HOWARD CUTLER

All that we are is the result of what we have thought. If a man speaks or acts with an evil thought, pain follows him. If a man speaks or acts with a pure thought, happiness follows him, like a shadow that never leaves him.

BUDDHA

We should be thankful to Buddhist and other spiritual teachers for showing us how to discover real happiness and be grateful for the kindness of others.

Accomplish small tasks as if they are great and noble. Learn to live happily in the present moment, to touch the peace and joy that are available now.

You know the basic rules: Care for your body as well as your ability and knowledge permit, and feed it the appropriate human food in the right amount.

The only true renunciation is to renounce seeking fulfillment in the fluttering phenomena of the world. The world becomes even more enjoyable once you stop demanding fulfillment from it.

Happiness is not a destination. It is a method of life.

Happiness cannot be found—it must be created anew everyday.

Pursue a livelihood that directly contributes to the well-being of the world and enables you to more fully use your competitive capacities.

Happiness comes from cultivating the virtues that lead to enlightenment, from wisdom and understanding the unchanging truth of change.

Feng shui says red, blue, or purple candles stimulate fame, fortune, reputation, happiness, festivity.

With ordinary talent and extraordinary perseverance, all things are attainable.

Nibbana (or nirvana) is the highest happiness,
beyond even the happiness of great insight or understanding,
because it transcends the mind itself. It is transforming. The
experience of nibbana has the power to uproot from the stream of
consciousness the unwholesome factors of mind that keep us bound to
samsara. The first moment of opening to the highest reality uproots
the attachment to self, to the sense of I. And it is said that from that
moment on, a being is destined to work through the remaining
defilements, such as greed and anger, on the way to full awakening.
JOSEPH GOLDSTEIN

Seek not happiness too greedily,
and be not fearful of unhappiness.
LAO-TZU

When we are not attached
to who we think we are, life can
move through us, playing us like
an instrument. Understanding
continual change, you release
your attempts to control
circumstances. Living in
an easy connection with life,
you live in joy.

If you want to be happy for an
hour, take a nap.

Live with no time out.

Awake, reflect, watch, work with
care and attention.

When we use really meaningful speech, people will listen. When it is kindly, people will be joyful. When it is polite, we will have many friends. When there is truthfulness, we can be relied on. When there is no slander or backbiting, we will be trusted.

Act as if it is your duty to be happy.

Reside at the center of the circle.

Our search for happiness is more often founded on our illusions than on reality.

The Buddha's teaching, therefore, is about achieving this freedom from suffering—ultimate happiness (though beyond what we might ordinarily conceive of as happiness).

Life is happening through you. When you get this, you might be able to truly enjoy work. You may be conscious of thoughts arising, but you are not those thoughts. You are the consciousness that is aware of the thoughts arising. You may be aware of work happening, but it is not being done by you, it is coming through you. You are the consciousness aware of the work.

Ask yourself: *What do I really want? Would I know it if I got it? Does everything have to be perfect or under my total control for me to be happy right now? Is everything basically okay right now? Am I just not noticing the ways in which things are good? Are there decisions or steps I can take that would move me toward peace and harmony?*

All of the Dharma is about lessening one's self absorption, one's ego-clinging. This brings you, and all beings, happiness.

Buddha's four things conducive to happiness: To be skilled, efficient, energetic, earnest, and learned in a profession. To conscientiously protect one's income and family's means of support. To have virtuous, trustworthy, and faithful friends and spiritual aspirations. To be content and live within one's means.

A moment comes when we realize that our life is the path.

Say nothing and saw wood.

Right mindfulness means working on being mindful all the time. Being mindful means being constantly aware of your feelings, your surroundings, what your own body is doing, what thoughts and ideas you are experiencing, and what is happening around you.

The Third Noble Truth is that suffering can be overcome and happiness can be attained; that true happiness and contentment are possible. If we give up useless craving and learn to live each day at a time (not dwelling in the past or the imagined future), then we can become happy and free. We then have more time and energy to help others. This is nirvana.

The horse in the field knows nothing of breakfast, lunch, and dinner. It eats when hungry. The point of Zen is to follow that same kind of naturalness.